James Joyce · Frank O'Connor
Liam O'Flaherty · Sean O'Faolain
Mary Lavin · Michael McLaverty

Great Irish Short Stories
Model Interpretations

By Noreen O'Donovan

in collaboration with Wolfgang Staeck

Ernst Klett Schulbuchverlag
Stuttgart Düsseldorf Berlin Leipzig

Acknowledgements

James Joyce, "An Encounter" from *Dubliners* (1914) is reprinted by permission of The Society of Authors, London, as literary representative of the Estate of James Joyce.

Frank O'Connor, "Guests of the Nation" from *Guests of the Nation* (1931) is reprinted by permission of A. D. Peters & Co. Ltd., London.

Liam O'Flaherty, "A Red Petticoat" from *The Short Stories of Liam O'Flaherty* (1937) is reprinted by permission of Jonathan Cape Ltd., London.

Sean O'Faolain, "The Man Who Invented Sin" from *The Man Who Invented Sin* (1948) is reprinted by kind permission of Curtis Brown Ltd., London, on behalf of the author.

Mary Lavin, "A Cup of Tea" from *The Long Ago and Other Stories* (1944) is reprinted by permission of the author.

Michael McLaverty, "Father Christmas" from *The Game Cock and Other Stories* (1947) is reprinted by permission of The Devin-Adair Company, Old Greenwich, Connecticut;

1. Auflage 1 8 7 | 2004 2003

Alle Drucke dieser Auflage können im Unterricht nebeneinander benutzt werden, sie sind untereinander unverändert. Die letzte Zahl bezeichnet das Jahr dieses Druckes.

Umschlaggestaltung: Hans Lämmle, Stuttgart.
Druck: Gutmann + Co, Heilbronn. Printed in Germany.
ISBN 3-12-579130-8

Contents

Introduction

Ireland's contribution to English Literature far exceeds what one would expect from the size of its population. This is all the more astonishing when one considers that it was only in the course of the 19th century that Irish gave way to English as the language of the majority. On the other hand, the influence of the older language and the Gaelic culture associated with it may well account for much of the vitality of Irish writing. The popularity of the short story in Ireland is, for example, often explained in terms of the oral story-telling tradition.

Whatever the reasons, it is an undeniable fact that practically all notable Irish writers of fiction have excelled in the shorter form, most of them preferring it to the novel. This has ensured a wide selection of stories to choose from for this collection. Since for most of our readers these stories will function as an introduction to Irish literature, we have chosen representative examples of the work of six of the country's most interesting and influential 20th-century authors.

At the same time, care has been taken to ensure that the themes and settings of the stories complement each other, to provide the reader with a balanced – though necessarily incomplete – picture of Irish society, as it has developed since the turn of the century. The political upheavals of the early decades and the search for national identity are reflected in the stories, as is the widespread sense of disillusionment with the kind of society which emerged after independence was achieved. The geographical settings range from the rugged west coast to the slums of Belfast. The struggle for a decent life under conditions of urban and rural poverty provides the background for two of the stories, whereas the characteristic atmosphere of a middle-class Irish family is evoked in another.

Some useful background information on the social context in which each of these stories was written will be found in the Biographical Notes on its author. Such information, together with all the other aids to comprehension we have included, is, of course, subordinate to the main aim of the collection: the reader's enjoyment of the stories themselves.

A Note on the Language

The English language was introduced to Ireland in the 13th century by the Anglo-Norman invaders . For several centuries it remained the language of a governing class, concentrated mainly in a small area along the east coast around Dublin. The decline of Irish (also referred to as Gaelic) began in the 17th century, after the defeat of the native Gaelic aristocracy. From then on, the use of English spread gradually westwards, partly as a result of a deliberate policy of cultural domination, and partly due to the identification of Irish with a defeated, impoverished race. The establishment of an independent state in 1921 came too late to turn the tide. Today, English is the vernacular in all but a few areas along the west coast.

The English spoken in Ireland – and thus the language of these stories – is basically standard English. It is, however, to a greater or lesser extent influenced by the older language. This influence is the least evident in the works of those writers from the east coast and the midlands, such as James Joyce and Mary Lavin – especially when they are writing about middle-class society. But even here, the sounds of the language when spoken would be recognizably Irish (the letter *r* pronounced in all positions; purer, less diphthongized vowels – [o:] instead of [əʊ], [e:] instead of [eɪ], [eə], etc.).

Those writers who come from other parts of Ireland, especially the south and west, are more likely to use forms that are strongly influenced by Irish. These include special words which have been taken over from Irish (e.g. *loch,* p. 35, *bosthoon,* p. 41), the use of the Gaelic diminutive *-een (houseen,* p. 23), the tendency to use *ye* as a plural of *you* (pp. 23, 28), structures which are direct translations from the Irish (e.g. *Is it ... you are?* p. 30), and occasional modifications of pronunciation in dialogue (*shpit,* p. 37, *divil,* p. 14). In the story by the bilingual author Liam O'Flaherty, most of the dialogue and a lot of the narrative sounds as if it were directly translated from Irish. This is a deliberate effect here, and does not make the story difficult to read or understand.

In the "Annotations" to each story, all deviations from standard British usage are marked as such. The following abbreviations are used:

Ir.	Irish usage	*coll.*	colloquial
Gael.	Gaelic (Irish language)	*sl.*	slang
Engl.	English (as opposed to Irish) usage	*dial.*	local dialect
Am.	American	*lit.*	literary
Scot.	Scottish	*vulg.*	vulgar

A Note to Teachers

Though each of these stories can be dealt with separately in class, the sequence in which they are here presented is not accidental. It is rather designed to enable students to develop a sense of time and place, a sense of the social reality underlying these Irish short stories. Hence the roughly chronological sequence.

Thus the Joyce story at the beginning of the sequence conveys something of the stagnation and frustation of 'pre-revolutionary' Dublin. What Joyce ignored – or even consciously rejected – was the cultural renaissance which accompanied the growth of Irish national consciousness at the turn of the century. Since this 'rebirth' of the Irish nation found its literary expression mainly in poetry and drama and not in the private, introspective art of the short story, it can be represented only indirectly in our collection: Frank O'Connor's famous "Guests of the Nation", though set in the fight for Irish independence, takes its mood of disenchantment from the thirties, when it was written.

The story by Liam O'Flaherty is intended to give an impression of what the struggle for independence was all about – the attempt to save an oppressed but still vivid native culture from total extinction. In itself it also demonstrates an important element in this Gaelic culture: the oral story-telling tradition, which contributed so much to the development of the modern Irish short story. The O'Faolain story has as its background the search for national and cultural 'roots', and contains a suggestion that one kind of oppression was merely exchanged for another.

The two final stories are less dependent on a fixed sequence for their full appreciation, but are nevertheless best dealt with after the social perspective has been established by reading at least some of the previous stories. In this way it should become clear that the very universality of these stories springs from their authors' absolute fidelity to the local and the specific.

Modification of this sequence may be called for in certain circumstances. If, for example, these stories are to function as an introduction to the short story as such, it would be inadvisable to start with the rather sophisticated and subtle Joyce story – this could either be omitted or dealt with at the end of the course. A reduced, but still plausible course in the Irish short story could consist of the O'Connor and O'Flaherty stories, plus Lavin *or* O'Faolain *or* McLaverty, possibly augmented by non-fictional material.

Suggestions for constructing other literary and thematic courses based on the individual stories are given at the end of the Teaching Notes on each story. These can alternatively be taken as suggestions for individual or group projects, or for private reading on the part of teachers or students. For those who would like to extend their knowledge of the Irish short story beyond this introduction to the 'classic' 20th-century authors, an additional reading list is given, which covers the 19th-century Anglo-Irish and Celtic antecedents as well as contemporary authors.

The Teaching Notes present in each case one of many possible approaches, but one which is intended to approximate a 'natural' reading of the story in question. By this we mean that instead of spending three or more lessons dissecting a story that is assumed to have been read and understood in advance, at least the first two units should accompany the students in their gradual discovery of what the story is all about. Where at all possible, the initial reading of the story has been divided into two parts. Where the structure of the story makes such a procedure inadvisable, the first two lessons still cover all that is necessary for a satisfactory reading of the story. The third unit is then devoted to an aspect which, while not essential for an appreciation of the story as fiction, adds a dimension of understanding; in most cases, this unit links the story with its social background.

Another guiding principle has been the primacy of the reader's personal response. Hence very sparing use has been made in the Teaching Notes of literary terminology which might suggest a mechanical application of categories instead of an honest reaction. Such terms are only introduced when a communicative need to use them can be assumed to have arisen. (This should not, of course, prevent any class already versed in the use of such terms from using them right from the start.) If the students' reaction to a story is very different from what is anticipated here, it should nevertheless be respected, and the teaching strategy modified accordingly. An obviously mistaken interpretation can in most cases be corrected by a close reading of the text.

Introductory Lesson (optional)

This introductory lesson is designed to supply some useful background information which will make many of the stories more easily accessible to the students and reduce their dependence on the annotations. It is based on a selection of slides from the series *Dias zur Landeskunde* (Klettnummer 56815). Since the *Lehrerheft* (Klettnummer 5681) gives all the necessary information on each of these slides, the following notes are restricted to suggestions as to procedure. It should be understood that on presenting each slide (or pair of slides), the teacher should first allow for the students' spontaneous reactions, remarks and questions before providing any information.

a) *Preliminary Discussion:* Intention to read some short stories by Irish authors – present knowledge about Ireland (or lack of it) – stories as source of information – some background knowledge an aid to understanding.

b) *The Celts and Celtic Culture*
Slides [7] Celtic Stone Figures
[19] Singing Pub
Procedure: Each slide shown briefly, for short comparison – obvious differences (stones/people, dead/alive, past/present); then each slide separately for information on the Celts and what remains of their culture today.

c) *Religion*
Slides [8] Clonmacnoise
[24] Croagh Patrick
Procedure: Short comparison – connection more obvious; then each slide separately for information on the importance of religion in Ireland, and especially the political and social significance of the Catholic Church.

d) *Regional Differences*
Slides [20] Farming on the Aran Islands
[27] Shipbuilding in Belfast
Procedure: Sum up differences, making clear that these pictures represent two extremes; then information on the economic and political neglect of the West (as opposed to the Midlands and East) and the industrialization of the North-East (reference to earlier confiscation of lands and Protestant 'plantations').

e) *Geography*

Slide [1] Map of Ireland

Refer back to the regional differences mentioned under d); point out the present political partition of the country, and the location of Dublin.

f) *Past and Present*

Slide [3] Dublin: O'Connell Street

Points: Centre of British power – rebellions – capital of independent republic.

Slide [13] Bilingual Signpost

Points: The language of the Celts (→[7]); spoken in Gaeltacht areas (→[20]); official policy in the Republic to preserve the language (→[3]); influence of Irish on English as spoken in Ireland (→ Stories, cf. 'A Note on the Language', p. 6).

James Joyce

An Encounter

It was Joe Dillon who introduced the Wild West to us. He had a little library made up of old numbers of *The Union Jack, Pluck,* and *The Halfpenny Marvel.* Every evening after school we met in his back garden and arranged Indian battles. He and his fat young brother Leo, the idler, held the loft of the stable while we tried to carry it by storm; or we fought a pitched battle on the grass. But, however well we fought, we never won siege or battle and all our bouts ended with Joe Dillon's war dance of victory. His parents went to eight o'clock mass every morning in Gardiner Street and the peaceful odour of Mrs Dillon was prevalent in the hall of the house. But he played too fiercely for us who were younger and more timid. He looked like some kind of an Indian when he capered round the garden, an old tea-cosy on his head, beating a tin with his fist and yelling:

"Ya! Yaka, yaka, yaka!"

Everyone was incredulous when it was reported that he had a vocation for the priesthood. Nevertheless it was true.

A spirit of unruliness diffused itself among us and, under its influence, differences of culture and constitution were waived. We banded ourselves together, some boldly, some in jest and some almost in fear: and of the number of these latter, the reluctant Indians who were afraid to seem studious or lacking in robustness, I was one. The adventures related in the literature of the Wild West were remote from my nature but, at least, they opened doors of escape. I liked better some American detective stories which were traversed from time to time by unkempt fierce and beautiful girls. Though there was nothing wrong in these stories and though their intention was sometimes literary, they were circulated secretly at school. One day when Father Butler was hearing the four pages of Roman History, clumsy Leo Dillon was discovered with a copy of *The Halfpenny Marvel.*

"This page or this page? This page? Now, Dillon, up. *Hardly had the day* ... Go on! What day? *Hardly had the day dawned* ... Have you studied it? What have you there in your pocket?"

Everyone's heart palpitated as Leo Dillon handed up the paper and everyone assumed an innocent face. Father Butler turned over the pages, frowning.

"What is this rubbish?" he said. "*The Apache Chief!* Is this what you read instead of studying your Roman History? Let me not find any more of this wretched stuff in this college. The man who wrote it, I suppose, was some wretched fellow who writes these things for a drink. I'm surprised at boys like you, educated, reading such stuff! I could understand it if you were ... National School boys. Now, Dillon, I advise you strongly, get at your work or ..."

This rebuke during the sober hours of school paled much of the glory of the Wild West for me, and the confused puffy face of Leo Dillon awakened one of my consciences. But when the restraining influence of the school was at a distance I began to hunger again for wild sensations, for the escape which these chronicles of disorder alone seemed to offer me. The mimic warfare of the evening became at last as wearisome to me as the routine of school in the morning because I wanted real adventures to happen to myself. But real adventures, I reflected, do not happen to people who remain at home: they must be sought abroad.

The summer holidays were near at hand when I made up my mind to break out of the weariness of school life for one day at least. With Leo Dillon and a boy named Mahony I planned a day's miching. Each of us saved up sixpence. We were to meet at ten in the morning on the Canal Bridge. Mahony's big sister was to write an excuse for him and Leo Dillon was to tell his brother to say he was sick. We arranged to go along the Wharf Road until we came to the ships, then to cross in the ferryboat and walk out to see the Pigeon House. Leo Dillon was afraid we might meet Father Butler or someone out of the college; but Mahony asked, very sensibly, what would Father Butler be doing out at the Pigeon House. We were reassured, and I brought the first stage of the plot to an end by collecting sixpence from the other two, at the same time showing them my own sixpence. When we were making the last arrangements on the eve we were all vaguely excited. We shook hands, laughing, and Mahony said:

"Till tomorrow, mates."

That night I slept badly. In the morning I was firstcomer to the bridge, as I lived nearest. I hid my books in the long grass near the ashpit at the end of the garden where nobody ever came, and hurried along the canal bank. It was a mild sunny morning in the first week of June. I sat up on the coping of the bridge, admiring my frail canvas shoes which I had diligently pipeclayed overnight and watching the docile horses pulling a tramload of business people up the hill. All the branches of the tall trees which lined the mall were gay with little light green leaves, and the sunlight slanted through them on to the water. The granite stone of the bridge was beginning to be warm, and I began to pat it with my hands in time to an air in my head. I was very happy.

When I had been sitting there for five or ten minutes I saw Mahony's grey suit approaching. He came up the hill, smiling, and clambered up beside me on the bridge. While we were waiting he brought out the catapult which bulged from his inner pocket and explained some improvements which he had made in it. I asked him why he had brought it, and he told me he had brought it to have some gas with the birds. Mahony used slang freely, and spoke of Father Butler as Old Bunser. We waited on for a quarter of an hour more, but still there was no sign of Leo Dillon. Mahony, at last, jumped down and said:

"Come along. I knew Fatty'd funk it."

"And his sixpence . . ." I said.

"That's forfeit," said Mahony. "And so much the better for us – a bob and a tanner instead of a bob."

We walked along the North Strand Road till we came to the Vitriol Works and then turned to the right along the Wharf Road. Mahony began to play the Indian as soon as we were out of public sight. He chased a crowd of ragged girls, brandishing his unloaded catapult and, when two ragged boys began, out of chivalry, to fling stones at us, he proposed that we should charge them. I objected that the boys were too small, and so we walked on, the ragged troop screaming after us "*Swaddlers! Swaddlers!*" thinking that we were Protestants because Mahony, who was dark-complexioned, wore the silver badge of a cricket club in his cap. When we came to the Smoothing Iron we arranged a siege; but it was a failure because you must have at least three. We revenged ourselves on Leo Dillon by saying what a funk he was and guessing how many he would get at three o'clock from Mr Ryan.

We came then near the river. We spent a long time walking about the noisy streets flanked by high stone walls, watching the working of cranes and engines and often being shouted at for our immobility by the drivers of groaning carts. It was noon when we reached the quays and, as all the labourers seemed to be eating their lunches, we bought two big currant buns and sat down to eat them on some metal piping beside the river. We pleased ourselves with the spectacle of Dublin's commerce – the barges signalled from far away by their curls of woolly smoke, the brown fishing fleet beyond Ringsend, the big white sailing vessel which was being discharged on the opposite quay. Mahony said it would be right skit to run away to sea on one of those big ships, and even I, looking at the high masts, saw, or imagined, the geography which had been scantily dosed to me at school gradually taking substance under my eyes. School and home seemed to recede from us and their influences upon us seemed to wane.

We crossed the Liffey in the ferryboat, paying our toll to be transported in the company of two labourers and a little Jew with a bag. We were serious to the point of solemnity, but once during the short voyage our eyes met and we laughed. When we landed we watched the discharging of the graceful three-master which we had observed from the other quay. Some bystander said that she was a Norwegian vessel. I went to the stern and tried to decipher the legend upon it but, failing to do so, I came back and examined the foreign sailors to see had any of them green eyes, for I had some confused notion ... The sailor's eyes were blue, and grey, and even black. The only sailor whose eyes could have been called green was a tall man who amused the crowd on the quay by calling out cheerfully every time the planks fell:

"All right! All right!"

When we were tired of this sight we wandered slowly into Ringsend. The day had grown sultry, and in the windows of the grocers' shops musty biscuits lay bleaching. We bought some biscuits and chocolate, which we ate sedulously as we wandered through the squalid streets where the families of the fishermen live. We could find no dairy and so we went into a huckster's shop and bought a bottle of raspberry lemonade each. Refreshed by this, Mahony chased a cat down a lane, but the cat escaped into a wide field. We both felt rather tired, and when we reached the field we made at once for a sloping bank, over the ridge of which we could see the Dodder.

It was too late and we were too tired to carry out our project of visiting the Pigeon House. We had to be home before four o'clock, lest our adventure should be discovered. Mahony looked regretfully at his catapult, and I had to suggest going home by train before he regained any cheerfulness. The sun went in behind some clouds and left us to our jaded thoughts and the crumbs of our provisions.

There was nobody but ourselves in the field. When we had lain on the bank for some time without speaking I saw a man approaching from the far end of the field. I watched him lazily as I chewed one of those green stems on which girls tell fortunes. He came along by the bank slowly. He walked with one hand upon his hip and in the other hand he held a stick with which he tapped the turf lightly. He was shabbily dressed in a suit of greenish-black and wore what we used to call a jerry hat with a high crown. He seemed to be fairly old, for his moustache was ashen-grey. When he passed at our feet he glanced up at us quickly and then continued his way. We followed him with our eyes and saw that when he had gone on for perhaps fifty paces he turned about and began to retrace his steps. He walked towards us very slowly, always tapping the ground with his stick, so slowly that I thought he was looking for something in the grass.

He stopped when he came level with us, and bade us good-day. We answered him, and he sat down beside us on the slope slowly and with great care. He began to talk of the weather, saying that it would be a very hot summer and adding that the seasons had changed greatly since he was a boy – a long time ago. He said that the happiest time of one's life was undoubtedly one's schoolboy days, and that he would give anything to be young again. While he expressed these sentiments, which bored us a little, we kept silent. Then he began to talk of school and of books. He asked us whether we had read the poetry of Thomas Moore or the works of Sir Walter Scott and Lord Lytton. I pretended that I had read every book he mentioned, so that in the end he said:

"Ah, I can see you are a bookworm like myself. Now," he added, pointing to Mahony, who was regarding us with open eyes, "he is different; he goes in for games."

He said he had all Sir Walter Scott's works and all Lord Lytton's works at home and never tired of reading them. "Of course," he said, there were some of Lord Lytton's works which boys couldn't read." Mahony asked why couldn't boys read them – a question which agitated and pained me because I was afraid the man would think I was a stupid as Mahony. The man, however, only smiled. I saw that he had great gaps in his mouth between his yellow teeth. Then he asked us which of us had the most sweethearts. Mahony mentioned lightly that he had three totties. The man asked me how many I had. I answered that I had none. He did not believe me and said he was sure I must have one. I was silent.

"Tell us," said Mahony pertly to the man, "how many have you yourself?"

The man smiled as before and said that when he was our age he had lots of sweethearts.

"Every boy," he said "has a little sweetheart."

His attitude on this point struck me as strangely liberal in a man of his age. In my heart I thought that what he said about boys and sweethearts was reasonable. But I disliked the words in his mouth, and I wondered why he shivered once or twice as if he feared something or felt a sudden chill. As he proceeded I noticed that his accent was good. He began to speak to us about girls, saying what nice soft hair they had and how soft their hands were and how all girls were not so good as they seemed to be if one only knew. There was nothing he liked, he said, so much as looking at a nice young girl, at her nice white hands and her beautiful soft hair. He gave me the impression that he was repeating something which he had learned by heart or that, magnetized by some words of his own speech, his mind was slowly circling round and round in the same orbit. At times he spoke as if he were simply alluding to some fact that everybody knew, and at times he lowered his voice and spoke mysteriously, as if he were telling us something secret which he did not wish others to overhear. He repeated his phrases over and over again, varying them and surrounding them with his monotonous voice. I continued to gaze towards the foot of the slope, listening to him.

After a long while his monologue paused. He stood up slowly, saying that he had to leave us for a minute or so, a few minutes, and, without changing the direction of my gaze, I saw him walking slowly away from us towards the near end of the field. We remained silent when he had gone. After a silence of a few minutes I heard Mahony exclaim:

"I say! Look what he's doing!"

As I neither answered nor raised my eyes, Mahony exclaimed again:

"I say ... He's a queer old josser!"

"In case he asks us for our names," I said, "let you be Murphy and I'll be Smith."

We said nothing further to each other. I was still considering whether I would go away or not when the man came back and sat down beside us again. Hardly had he sat down when Mahony, catching sight of the cat which had escaped him, sprang up and pursued her across the field. The man and I watched the chase. The cat escaped once more and Mahony began to throw stones at the wall she had escaladed. Desisting from this, he began to wander about the far end of the field, aimlessly.

After an interval the man spoke to me. He said that my friend was a very rough boy, and asked did he get whipped often at school. I was going to reply indignantly that we were not National School boys to be whipped, as he called it; but I remained silent. He began to speak on the subject of chastising boys. His mind, as if magnetized again by his speech, seemed to circle slowly round and round its new centre. He said that when boys were that kind they ought to be whipped and well whipped. When a boy was rough and unruly there was nothing would do him any good but a good sound whipping. A slap on the hand or a box on the ear was no good: what he wanted was to get a nice warm whipping. I was surprised at this sentiment and involuntarily glanced at his face. As I did so I met the gaze of a pair of bottle-green eyes peering at me from under a twitching forehead. I turned my eyes away again.

The man continued his monologue. He seemed to have forgotten his recent liberalism. He said that if ever he found a boy talking to girls or having a girl for a sweetheart he would whip him and whip him; and that would teach him not to be talking to girls. And if a boy had a girl for a sweetheart and told lies about it, then he would give him such a whipping as no boy ever got in this world. He said that there was nothing in this world he would like so well as that. He described to me how he would whip such a boy, as if he were unfolding some elaborate mystery. He would love that, he said, better than anything in this world; and his voice, as he led me monotonously through the mystery, grew almost affectionate and seemed to plead with me that I should understand him.

I waited till his monologue paused again. Then I stood up abruptly. Lest I should betray my agitation I delayed a few moments, pretending to fix my shoe properly, and then, saying that I was obliged to go, I bade him goodday. I went up the slope calmly but my heart was beating quickly with fear that he would seize me by the ankles. When I reached the top of the slope I turned round and, without looking at him, called loudly across the field:

"Murphy!"

My voice had an accent of forced bravery in it, and I was ashamed of my paltry stratagem. I had to call the name again before Mahony saw me and hallooed in answer. How my heart beat as he came running across the field to me! He ran as if to bring me aid. And I was penitent; for in my heart I had always despised him a little.

Biographical Notes

James Joyce was born in Dublin in 1882. He was educated mainly at a renowned Jesuit school, where he showed considerable interest in languages and literature. He went on to study languages and philosophy at the Dublin college of what was then the Royal University. His first published work was a review of an Ibsen play in a literary magazine – because of his interest in this writer he had even learnt Norwegian.

As well as consuming vast amounts of European literature, Joyce was also familiar with Irish literature, folklore, and language. However, he rejected the cultural and political nationalism that was spreading among his fellow-students, for what he saw as its narrowness and bigotry. He also became alienated from the Catholic Church, though he had at one point considered becoming a priest. His youthful conflicts are described in his autobiographical novel A Portrait of the Artist as a Young Man.

At the age of 22 he got married and left Ireland with his wife to live on the

Continent. He only returned for short visits after that. In the same year as he left Ireland, he began writing the stories that were to be published ten years later as Dubliners. *(The delay was due to the publishers' objections: one of the stories they wanted changed or omitted was "An Encounter".) His stated intention was to write "a chapter of the moral history of my country", concentrating on Dublin as the centre of what he called its "paralysis".*

In his years working as a language teacher in Trieste, Zurich and later Paris, Joyce went on to write two novels which are universally regarded as masterpieces: Ulysses *and* Finnegans Wake. *Though the stylistic innovations of these novels had a great impact on modern literature, they were constructed out of the same material as his earliest stories: the concrete detail of everyday life in Dublin. James Joyce died in Zurich in 1941.*

Annotations

5 **encounter** (unexpected) meeting – 2 **The Union Jack ... Marvel** cheap magazines for boys, specializing in adventure stories – 4 **to idle** to do nothing, to be lazy – **loft** room under the roof – 5 **stable** building for horses – **to carry by storm** to capture in a battle – **pitched battle** one fought by organized armies – 6 **siege** [i:] surrounding of an enemy to make them surrender – 7 **bout** [aʊ] fight (especially in boxing) – 9 **odour** ['əʊdə(r)] smell – **prevalent** present everywhere – 11 **to caper** to dance or run around – **tea-cosy** woollen cover for a tea-pot – 14 **to be incredulous** not to believe something – **vocation** calling; feeling of duty to take up a religious or social profession – 16 **unruliness** disregard for rules; wild behaviour – **to diffuse** to spread – 17 **to waive** to disregard – 18 **in jest** as a joke, for fun – 19 **reluctant** unwilling – 21 **remote** distant, far away – 23 **to traverse** to cross; *here:* to come up in a story – **unkempt** untidy – 31 **to palpitate** to beat fast – 32 **to assume** *here:* to put on

6 3 **wretched** ['––] of bad quality, pitiful – 6 **National School** state school for children aged 5–14 (as opposed to the private secondary school the boys went to) – 8 **rebuke** disapproving remark – **to pale** *here:* to make seem less interesting – 9 **puffy** very fat – 10 **to restrain** to hold back – 12 **chronicle** written record of events – **mimic** imitation, not real – 13 **wearisome** boring – 19 **Mahony** ['mæhənɪ] – **to mich** *(or* **mitch***) Ir. sl.* to play truant, to stay away from school – 22 **wharf** [ɔ:] docks – 24 **Pigeon House** a power station on a peninsula extending into Dublin Bay (named after its builder) – 27 **to be reassured** to feel secure again – 31 **mate** friend (Kumpel) – 33 **ash-pit** hole in the ground filled with ashes – 35 **coping** stonework on top of a wall – 36 **frail** light, easily damaged – **canvas** heavy cloth used for shoes, sails, tents etc. – **diligent** willing to work – **pipeclay** substance used to make tennis shoes white (and for making pipes) – 37 **docile** ['dɒsaɪl] obedient, quiet – 38 **mall** avenue

7 4 **to clamber** to climb – 6 **to bulge** to press (cloth, etc.) out of shape by taking up too much space – 8 **gas** *Ir. sl.* fun – 12 **to funk** to lack courage, to 'get cold feet' – 14 **forfeit**

['fɔ:(r)fət] given up as a consequence of the rules, or as punishment – **bob** shilling – 15 **tanner** sixpence (both old currency) – 19 **to brandish** to hold up or wave in the air – **to fling** to throw – 22 **swaddler** [ɒ] *dated sl.* Protestant – 23 **dark-complexioned** with rather dark skin – 24 **cricket** English game, played in Ireland only by Protestants of English descent – **the Smoothing Iron** flat stone in the shape of an iron (Bügeleisen) at the entrance to a bathing place on the south side of Dublin (no longer in existence because land has been reclaimed from the sea at this point) – 27 **how many (slaps) he would get** how much punishment ... – 33 **currant bun** little cake containing dried fruits – 35 **barge** long flat boat for carrying heavy goods (coal, etc.) – 37 **Ringsend** poor part of Dublin just south of the Liffey estuary – **vessel** ship – **to discharge** *here:* to unload – 38 **a right skit** *Ir. sl.* great fun – 40 **scantily** in small quantities – **to dose** [s] to give in exactly measured quantities

8 1 **to recede** to move away into the distance – 2 **to wane** to fade, to lose strength – 3 **toll** *here:* fare – 5 **solemnity** great seriousness – 9 **to decipher** *here:* to read – 14 **planks** wood cut in long flat pieces – 17 **sultry** hot, close, sticky (weather) – **musty** stale, gone bad – **to bleach** to make white – 19 **sedulous** dutiful; working hard at s.th. – **squalid** [ɒ] miserable, dirty, poor – 20 **huckster** seller of all kinds of small goods – 24 **ridge** top edge – **Dodder** small river which flows northwards into the Liffey estuary – 29 **jaded** tired – 34 **to tell fortunes** to predict s.o.'s future

9 1 **pace** length of one step – **to retrace one's steps** to go back the same way – 12 **Thomas Moore** (1779–1852) Irish poet and song-writer – **Sir Walter Scott** (1771–1832) Scottish writer of romantic novels – 13 **Lord Lytton** (1803–1873) writer of novels whose contents (horror, crime) shocked many contemporaries – 21 **to agitate** to trouble, to make feel uncomfortable – 25 **totties** *Dublin sl.* girl friends – 28 **pertly** brightly, in a rather cheeky manner

10 4 **orbit** circle, like that of the moon round the earth – **to allude to** to refer to – 17 **josser** *sl.* old fool – 23 **to pursue** to follow – 25 **to escalade** *lit.* to climb – **to desist from** to stop – 28 **to whip, to chastise** to beat severely – 35 **box on the ear** slap on the side of a person's head – 38 **to twitch** to move involuntarily

11 10 **to plead** to ask for something urgently – 13 **to bid good day (bade** [æ], **bidden)** *here:* to say good-bye – 15 **to seize** to catch – 19 **paltry** [ɔ:] small, pitiful – **strategem** trick – 21 **penitent** sorry, regretful

Interpretation and Teaching Notes

Background, Content and Analysis

"An Encounter" is the second story in Joyce's *Dubliners*. Though each of the stories in this collection is complete in itself, they are thematically linked. As regards Joyce's intentions in writing these stories, we have his own statement:

My intention was to write a chapter of the moral history of my country, and I chose Dublin for the scene because that city seemed to me the centre of paralysis. I have tried to present it to the indifferent public under four of its aspects: childhood, adolescence, maturity and public life. The stories are arranged in this order.[1]

In this scheme of things, "An Encounter" can be seen to belong to the childhood section, which also includes the first and third stories. An even closer link between the first three stories of *Dubliners* is provided by the narrator, who in "An Encounter" seems to be aged about 12–14. The remaining twelve stories in *Dubliners,* from "Eveline" to "The Dead", are all in the form of third-person narratives, which suggests a greater distance between writer and protagonists.

The semi-autobiographical nature of the first three stories is well documented[2]. As regards "An Encounter", we have Stanislaus Joyce's account of a very similar incident in involving himself and his brother[3]. In addition, there is considerable internal evidence which links the boy narrator of this story with the semi-autobiographical figure of Stephen in *A Portrait of the Artist as a Young Man.* Our narrator is shown to be a similarly sensitive and intelligent boy somewhat ill at ease in his environment. The decisive difference being that – unlike Stephen – he remains a true Dubliner: he does not escape.

Escape, or rather the desire for it, could be termed the leitmotif of the story. The Wild West games described at the beginning of the story are, for the narrator, a means of imaginative escape (p. 5, ll. 20–22) from the dreariness of school life. This is something he shares with his class-mate Leo Dillon, Leo's elder brother Joe, and possibly with schoolboys everywhere.

1 Letter from James Joyce to the publisher Grant Richards, 5 May 1906; published in *Letters of James Joyce* Vol. II, ed. Stuart Gilbert

2 e.g. Joyce's letter to his brother Stanislaus Joyce, 24 September 1905; ibid.

3 Stanislaus Joyce, *My Brother's Keeper,* ed. Richard Ellman

Such games do not fully satisfy him, however, and fail to still his longing for "real adventures" (p. 6, ll. 10–16). He therefore plans a day's 'miching' from school with Leo Dillon and another boy named Mahony.

The reasons for the narrator's unease are hinted at in the first few pages of the story. The inadequacy of Wild West games is demonstrated by 'wild' Joe Dillon's decision to become a priest, in the pious tradition of his family. Though we are told that this surprised everybody, we see that there is no real contradiction between such games and conventional religion: not only do such games not save one from incorporation into the 'establishment', but as harmless outlets for everyday frustrations, they may even be seen as a necessary part of what our narrator is longing to escape from.

The nature of the establishment which has swallowed up Joe Dillon is exemplified by the boys' teacher, Father Butler. In his brief appearance (p. 5, l. 26 – p. 6, l. 7) he is amply condemned for his insensitivity and snobbery. Though the narrator seems to be aware of his teacher's mediocrity, he remains a figure of authority for him. The boy's vulnerability and impressionability is revealed by his reaction to the priest's rebuke (p. 6, ll. 8–10). This adds weight to his subsequent remark about adventures not happening to people who stay at home.

The exact nature of the "adventures" the boy seeks is not, of course, specified, as appropriate to the limited awareness of a 12–14-year-old boy. In his preference for American detective stories with their "fierce and beautiful girls" there is, however, a suggestion of emergent sexuality. This makes the actual outcome of the outing – a confrontation with a sordid, perverted version of adult sexuality – all the more disturbing.

The narrator's plan for the outing reflects his feeling that real adventures "must be sought abroad". They are to head towards the sea, towards the foreign ships, then cross the Liffey, and visit a power station at the end of a peninsula. But things do not turn out as planned. First of all, Leo Dillon fails to turn up at their meeting-point, having been timid and half-hearted from the start. Mahony gets involved in a ridiculous fight with some ragged children: for him, the outing is just a continuation of their usual games of 'cowboys and Indians'. Their attempt to stage a siege is a failure. For a while, the narrator seems to achieve some of the freedom he has been looking for (p. 6, l. 38 – p. 7, l. 2 and p. 7, l. 34 – p. 8, l. 2), but even here there is disillusionment and failure: he is surprised to find that sailors do not necessarily have green eyes; he also fails to decipher the name of the Norwegian ship.

All in all, one could describe the boys' outing as a series of minor failures. Because they have wasted so much time, they get no further east than the slums of Ringsend. There, they "could find no dairy" and soon it is "too late" and they are "too tired" to continue (p. 8, ll. 20–26). Before turning back, they take a rest in a field. Here the 'encounter' takes place which gives the story its name.

At first there is no indication that the encounter will be in any way unpleasant. The narrator is lazily chewing a "green stem" as he watches the man approach. One gets the impression that the explicit reference to the colour green is deliberately evocative of the positive connotations it held on p. 6, l. 39, and the notions of 'escape' and 'abroad' associated with it on p. 8, l. 10. If so, the man's shabby "greenish-black" suit may be a foreshadowing of what becomes of the narrator's dreams of escape.

After some initial, rather conventional remarks, the man goes on to talk about books, and soon has picked out the narrator as a kindred spirit, unlike Mahony, who obviously "goes in for games". The narrator does not object to this, and even seems to seek the man's approval by trying to live up to his expectations. In this he demonstrates some of the impressionability we noticed earlier in his reaction to Father Butler's rebuke. In contrast, Mahony's boyish impudence seems to save him from any deeper involvement with the man, who turns out to be some sort of sexual pervert.

The narrator is somewhat impressed by the man's "strangely liberal" talk of girls, but something in his manner is disturbing: he does not, of course, recognize the sexual nature of the man's tension (p. 9, ll. 35–36). When the man leaves them for a few minutes, only Mahony watches him. He is surprised, but not deeply affected by what is presumably an act of exhibitionism on the man's part, and soon goes back to chasing cats. The fact that the narrator deliberately does not look suggests that he is more deeply affected, and prefers to avoid a conscious acknowledgement of what he has sensed. His desire for (physical, spiritual and intellectual) escape and adventure has led him into a confrontation with a degraded version of escape from conventions. Surprised by the man's sudden outburst of sadistic fantasies he stares into the man's eyes, which are, appropriately, dark green. The narrator's unwillingness to accept his disillusionment and defeat shows in the length of time he lingers in the man's company. Then, rejecting the man's last attempt to win his sympathy, he flees to the safety of Mahony's healthy, unthinking normality.

The last sentence of the story not only implies a rejection of his own freedom. Linking our narrator with the semi-autobiographical 'artist' figures of Joyce's early fiction, one might say that the boy represents what may become of the sensitive and intelligent when they lack the strength and single-mindedness to break out of Dublin's paralysis. The symbolic ambivalence of the colour green (which is, incidentally, the traditional symbol of Ireland and Irish nationalism) suggests the difficulty of discerning true from illusory freedom in an Irish context. Thus the story as a whole can be understood as an indirect confirmation of something we heard quite early in the story: "real adventures", as the boy intuitively recognized, "must be sought abroad".

First Unit
The Narrator and His Dreams of Adventure

Preparation: The students should have read at least to page 8, line 30.

1. General impression of narrator
What impression do you get of the boy who is telling the story
- *in the first 7 lines?*
- *in the first paragraph?*
- *in the first page?*

Initial impression of a perfectly normal schoolboy, who likes playing cowboys and Indians – then identification with the more "timid" boys (ll. 10, 18–20); finally, an impression of a studious, intelligent and somewhat precocious boy who is afraid to seem 'different' (esp. ll. 20–25).

2. His description of the Dillon family
Sum up the information given about the Dillon family. Why do you think the narrator picks out these details?
Parents: devout Roman Catholics who go to mass every morning; Joe Dillon, the elder of the two boys, wild and unruly, but decides to become a priest; his younger brother Leo: quieter, lazy.
The narrator's reference to his friend's Wild West antics sounds quite natural for a schoolboy; his reference to their parents' piety seems completely irrelevant at first – until we are told of Joe's "vocation", and the general surprise this caused; we are not told whether the narrator himself was surprised.

3. His dreams of adventure
What is the boy narrator's attitude to the stories he reads? What does this reveal about him?
Wild West stories: remote from his nature (l. 21) – presumably their emphasis on violence and simplified black-and-white morality did not offer

enough intellectual and psychological interest to this studious and sensitive boy; but they "opened doors of escape" (l. 22) – which indicates some dissatisfaction with his present situation.
Detective stories: prefers these presumably because of their greater psychological interest; his reference to the "fierce and beautiful girls" suggests emergent sexual feelings.
Why does the narrator plan a day's "miching"? What is he looking for?
Reasons given (p. 6, ll. 11–18): desire for "wild sensations", "real adventures", "escape" from "the weariness of school life"; his remark that real adventures "do not happen to people who remain at home" is supported by his own reaction to Father Butler's rebuke (ll. 1–10) – in order to be really free he must get away from the teacher's influence for a while.

4. The boys' actual adventures: patterns of failure
Describe what the boys get up to while "miching" from school.
(p. 6, l. 32 – p. 8, l. 30) One boy, Leo Dillon, fails to turn up; Mahony and the narrator walk southward to the North Dublin docks, Mahony looking for someone to fight; they cross the Liffey in a ferryboat, admire a Norwegian ship, turn eastward towards Ringsend, don't get to the Pigeon House power station as intended.
How satisfying is the boys' "adventure" up to this point?
Not very; full of minor confusion and failures – attacked by small boys (p. 7, ll. 19–22), their siege is a failure (ll. 25–26), the narrator fails to decipher the name of the ship (p. 8, l. 9). However, the ships in the harbour encourage the narrator in his dreams of escape (p. 7, ll. 34 – p. 8. l. 2, cf. also p. 6, l. 16).

Homework: Read to end.

Second Unit
The Significance of the Encounter

1. The narrator's initial reactions to the stranger
Look closely at the passage from p. 8, l. 31 to p. 9, l. 27. How does the narrator react to the old man at first?
Cautious interest at first; he seems to be impressed by the man's intellectual pretensions – pretends to have read all the authors mentioned (p. 9, ll. 11–13), is anxious for the man's approval (ll. 21–22), etc.

2. His perception of the man's abnormality

To what extent does his attitude change after this? Consider in particular the passage up to p. 10, l. 19.

First indication of a change in attitude: the narrator's silence (p. 9, l. 27) in reaction to the man's question about "sweethearts"; though he agrees with the man's "liberal" sentiments, he "disliked the words in his mouth" (l. 35) possibly because he senses something strange about the man. He notices his shivering and his repetitive talk about girls (p. 10, ll. 1–9), without quite understanding the reason for this – though he is warned enough to prefer not to look (ll. 11–12, 16) when the man walks to the end of the field. (Though we are not told directly – in accordance with the limited point of view – the man turns out to be an exhibitionist.) By ll. 18–19 it has become clear that the boy is looking for a way out of the situation.

3. The narrator's alienation from his 'dreams'

Can you explain the narrator's confused feelings with regard to the old man (as already described, and as they are developed in the remainder of the story)?

The boy had probably unconsciously identified the man at first with his dreams of literature/sex/escape (see point 1 above); his gradual revulsion, and then his realization that the man is a sexual pervert, then amounts to a discrediting of such dreams. This would explain his indecision (p. 10, ll. 20–21) and his continuing to listen (p. 10, ll. 27 – p. 11, l. 10).

Why do you think the boy is so struck by the man's "bottle-green eyes" (p. 10, l. 38)?

Cf. p. 8, ll. 10–14: he had imagined that the foreign sailors would have green eyes – obviously connected with his ideas of escape/freedom/adventure; the pervert's green eyes might suggest to him that this is what 'escape' leads to.

4. The ending of the story

Describe the narrator's feelings at the end of the story. How does his attitude to Mahony change?

As he admits in the last line, and as already hinted at (p. 9, l. 22), the narrator had previously felt superior to his friend; now he turns to Mahony (who seems totally unaffected by the encounter) to get him out of the situation. He probably now feels there is safety in mediocrity and conformity.

Homework: Re-read the story, paying special attention to the author's use of concrete detail.

Third Unit
Dublin and the Irish Scene – as Reality and Symbol

1. The setting of the story

What kinds of concrete detail can you find in the first two pages of the story? What is its general effect?

Names of people, magazines, etc., give an impression of reality; these, combined with geographical and historical details (e.g. Gardiner Street, Wharf Road, horse-trams), serve to establish the setting clearly: Dublin at the turn of the century, Catholic middle-class milieu.

2. The narrator's attitude to his environment

What is the boy's attitude to the kind of society he lives in – and to his country?

Ambivalent: he seems to be a good student, respectful of authority – but longs to escape from "the weariness of school life", Father Butler's influence, etc. (cf. First Unit, point 3). In addition, he seems to identify Ireland with constriction and lack of freedom: adventures "must be sought abroad".

What circumstances in the story seem to support such a view?

The influence of the Catholic Church in Ireland is demonstrated through the references to the Dillon family (and especially the 'fate' of Joe Dillon), and in the person of Father Butler. Doubt is cast on the quality of such authority through the episode of Leo Dillon and *The Halfpenny Marvel* (p. 5, l. 24 – p. 6, l. 7): the narrator seems to possess a greater sensitivity and understanding of literature than his teacher.

3. Geographical and other symbols of 'escape'

What symbolic value can you find in the course the boys' outing takes?

Their plan: to go out to the Pigeon House at the end of a peninsula – which is as far east as one can go in Dublin; the notion 'eastwards/towards the sea/ away from Ireland' is identified with 'escape'. The boys' failure to reach the Pigeon House can be seen as a symbol of the narrator's failure to achieve real freedom.

Some critics think the author's references to certain colours have a symbolic significance. Can you find any such examples?

Most obvious – green, as a symbol of what the boy is looking for; positive associations on p. 6, l. 39 and p. 8, l. 33; on 'green eyes' as a symbol of 'freedom', see Second Unit, point 3. The reference to the pervert's "greenish-black" suit (p. 8, ll. 36–37) could be understood as a comment on a degraded Irish version of freedom. Note that green is itself traditionally a symbol of Ireland and Irish nationalism.

4. Joyce's view of the Irish 'paralysis'
[Quote, or present on blackboard/OH-projector, Joyce's statement on his intentions in writing *Dubliners* (see Background, Content and Analysis)] *To what extent has he achieved this in the story you have just read?*
Paralysis: the narrator's failure to achieve freedom, and his reversion to the safety of conformity at the end of the story. Since the story begins with an example of a spirited, unruly boy conforming to Irish society's expectations, and since this is echoed in the narrator's own experience, "paralysis" is made to seem like a general condition.

For Further Study

Points for discussion

1. Trace the course of the boys' outing on a map of Dublin.
2. Write a character sketch of Mahony.
3. [Discussion or written comment] Is the boy's resignation final?

Courses/Projects based on this story

1. James Joyce – a Portrait of the Artist
- From *Dubliners,* the stories "An Encounter", "Eveline" and possibly "The Dead"; the additional stories to be taken either from the Penguin paperback edition, or from the various school editions and anthologies available. ("Eveline" is widely anthologized, e. g. in *Great English Short Stories,* Klett; there is a Hueber school edition of "The Dead".) Alternatively, one could take the CVK selection of 5 stories.
- *A Portrait of the Artist as a Young Man* (Penguin or Heinemann/ Hirschgraben), or selected extracts, e.g. pp. 7–9, 50–52, 157–158, 201–203, 238–239 (page numbers refer to the Penguin edition)
- Examples of Joyce's later prose – short extracts from *Ulysses* and *Finnegans Wake*

2. Stories of Initiation
- At least three stories from the collection of the same name, edited by Wolfgang Staeck (Klett)
- "An Encounter" as a story of initiation

Frank O'Connor

Guests of the Nation

I

At dusk the big Englishman, Belcher, would shift his long legs out of the ashes and say "Well, chums, what about it?" and Noble and myself would say "All right, chum" (for we had picked up some of their curious expressions), and the little Englishman, Hawkins, would light the lamp and bring out the cards. Sometimes Jeremiah Donovan would come up and supervise the game, and get excited over Hawkins' cards, which he always played badly, and shout at him, as if he was one of our own, "Ah, you divil, why didn't you play the trey?"

But ordinarily Jeremiah was a sober and contented poor devil like the big Englishman Belcher, and was looked up to only because he was a fair hand at documents, though he was slow even with them. He wore a small cloth hat and big gaiters over his long pants, and you seldom saw him with his hands out of his pockets. He reddened when you talked to him, tilting from toe to heel and back, and looking down all the time at his big farmer's feet. Noble and myself used to make fun of his broad accent, because we were both from the town.

I could not at the time see the point of myself and Noble guarding Belcher and Hawkins at all, for it was my belief that you could have planted that pair down anywhere from this to Claregalway and they'd have taken root there like a native weed. I never in my short experience saw two men take to the country as they did.

They were passed on to us by the Second Battalion when the search for them became too hot, and Noble and myself, being young, took them over with a natural feeling of responsibility, but Hawkins made us look like fools when he showed that he knew the country better than we did.

"You're the bloke they call Bonaparte," he says to me. "Mary Brigid O'Connell told me to ask what you'd done with the pair of her brother's socks you borrowed."

For it seemed, as they explained it, that the Second had little evenings, and some of the girls of the neighbourhood turned up, and seeing they were such decent chaps, our fellows could not leave the two Englishmen out. Hawkins learned to dance "The Walls of Limerick", "The Siege of Ennis" and "The Waves of Tory" as well as any of them, though he could not return the compliment, because our lads that time did not dance foreign dances on principle.

So whatever privileges Belcher and Hawkins had with the Second they just took naturally with us, and after the first couple of days we gave up all pretence of keeping an eye on them. Not that they could have got far, because they had accents you could cut with a knife, and wore khaki tunics and overcoats with civilian pants and boots, but I believe myself they never had any idea of escaping and were quite content to be where they were.

It was a treat to see how Belcher got off with the old woman in the house where we were staying. She was a great warrant to scold, and cranky even with us, but before ever she had a chance of giving our guests, as I may call them, a lick of her tongue, Belcher had made her his friend for life. She was breaking sticks, and Belcher, who had not been more than ten minutes in the house, jumped up and went over to her.

"Allow me, madam," he said, smiling his queer little smile. "Please allow me," and he took the hatchet from her. She was too surprised to speak, and after that, Belcher would be at her heels, carrying a bucket, a basket or a load of turf. As Noble said, he got into looking before she leapt, and hot water, or any little thing she wanted, Belcher would have ready for her. For such a huge man (and though I am five foot ten myself I had to look up at him) he had an uncommon lack of speech. It took us a little while to get used to him, walking in and out like a ghost, without speaking. Especially because Hawkins talked enough for a platoon, it was strange to hear Belcher with his toes in the ashes come out with a solitary "Excuse me, chum," or "That's right, chum." His one and only passion was cards, and he was a remarkably good card player. He could have skinned myself and Noble, but whatever we lost to him, Hawkins lost to us, and Hawkins only played with the money Belcher gave him.

Hawkins lost to us because he had too much old gab, and we probably lost to Belcher for the same reason. Hawkins and Noble argued about religion into the early hours of the morning, and Hawkins worried the life out of Noble, who had a brother a priest, with a string of questions that would puzzle a cardinal. Even in treating of holy subjects, Hawkins had a deplorable tongue. I never met a man who could mix such a variety of cursing and bad language into any argument. He was a terrible man, and a fright to argue. He never did a stroke of work, and when he had no one else to argue with, he got stuck in the old woman.

He met his match in her, for when he tried to get her to complain profanely of the drought she gave him a great comedown by blaming it entirely on Jupiter Pluvius (a deity neither Hawkins nor I had ever heard of, though Noble said that among the pagans it was believed that he had something to do with the rain). Another day he was swearing at the capitalists for starting the German war when the old lady laid down her iron, puckered up her little crab's mouth and said: "Mr Hawkins, you can say what you like about the war, and think you'll deceive me because I'm only a simple poor countrywoman, but I know what started the war. It was the Italian Count that stole the heathen divinity out of the temple of Japan. Believe me, Mr. Hawkins, nothing but sorrow and want can follow people who disturb the hidden powers."

A queer old girl, all right.

II

One evening we had our tea and Hawkins lit the lamp and we all sat into cards. Jeremiah Donovan came in too, and sat and watched us for a while, and it suddenly struck me that he had no great love for the two Englishmen. It came as a surprise to me because I had noticed nothing of it before.

Late in the evening a really terrible argument blew up between Hawkins and Noble about capitalists and priests and love of country.

"The capitalists pay the priests to tell you about the next world so that you won't notice what the bastards are up to in this," said Hawkins.

"Nonsense, man!" said Noble, losing his temper. "Before ever a capitalist was thought of people believed in the next world."

Hawkins stood up as though he was preaching.

"Oh, they did, did they?" he said with a sneer. "They believed all the things you believe – isn't that what you mean? And you believe God created Adam, and Adam created Shem, and Shem created Jehoshophat. You believe all that silly old fairytale about Eve and Eden and the apple. Well listen to me, chum! If you're entitled to a silly belief like that, I'm entitled to my own silly belief – which is that the first thing your God created was a bleeding capitalist, with morality and Rolls-Royce complete. Am I right, chum?" he says to Belcher.

"You're right, chum," says Belcher with a smile, and he got up from the table to stretch his long legs into the fire and stroke his moustache. So, seeing that Jeremiah Donovan was going, and that there was no knowing when the argument about religion would be over, I went out with him. We strolled down to the village together, and then he stopped, blushing and mumbling, and said I should be behind, keeping guard. I didn't like the tone he took with me, and anyway I was bored with life in the cottage, so I replied by asking what the hell we wanted to guard them for at all.

He looked at me in surprise and said: "I thought you knew we were keeping them as hostages."

"Hostages?" I said.

"The enemy have prisoners belonging to us, and now they're talking of shooting them," he said. "If they shoot our prisoners, we'll shoot theirs."

"Shoot Belcher and Hawkins?" I said.

"What else did you think we were keeping them for?" he said.

"Wasn't it very unforeseen of you not to warn Noble and myself of that in the beginning?" I said.

"How was it?" he said. "You might have known that much."

"We could not know it, Jeremiah Donovan," I said. "How could we when they were on our hands so long?"

"The enemy have our prisoners as long and longer," he said.

"That's not the same thing, at all," said I.

"What difference is there?" said he.

I couldn't tell him, because I knew he wouldn't understand. If it was only an old dog that you had to take to the vet's, you'd try and not get too fond of him, but Jeremiah Donovan was not a man who would ever be in danger of that.

"And when is this to be decided?" I said.

"We might hear tonight," he said. "Or tomorrow or the next day at latest. So if it's only hanging round that's a trouble to you, you'll be free soon enough."

It was not the hanging round that was a trouble to me at all by this time. I had worse things to worry about. When I got back to the cottage the argument was still on. Hawkins was holding forth in his best style, maintaining that there was no next world, and Noble saying that there was; but I could see that Hawkins had had the best of it.

"Do you know what, chum?" he was saying with a saucy smile. "I think you're just as big a bleeding unbeliever as I am. You say you believe in the next world, and you know just as much about the next world as I do, which is sweet damn-all. What's heaven? You don't know. Where's heaven? You don't know. You know sweet damn-all! I ask you again, do they wear wings?"

"Very well, then," said Noble. "They do. Is that enough for you? They do wear wings."

"Where do they get them then? Who makes them? Have they a factory for wings? Have they a sort of store where you hand in your chit and take your bleeding wings?"

"You're an impossible man to argue with," said Noble. "Now, listen to me –" And they were off again.

It was long after midnight when we locked up and went to bed. As I blew out the candle I told Noble. He took it very quietly. When we'd been in bed about an hour he asked if I thought we should tell the Englishmen. I didn't, because I doubted if the English would shoot our men. Even if they did, the Brigade officers, who were always up and down to the Second Battalion and knew the Englishmen well, would hardly want to see them plugged. "I think so too," said Noble. "It would be great cruelty to put the wind up them now."

"It was very unforeseen of Jeremiah Donovan, anyhow," said I.

It was next morning that we found it so hard to face Belcher and Hawkins. We went about the house all day, scarcely saying a word. Belcher didn't seem to notice; he was stretched into the ashes as usual, with his usual look of waiting in quietness for something unforeseen to happen, but Hawkins noticed it and put it down to Noble being beaten in the argument of the night before.

"Why can't you take the discussion in the proper spirit?" he said severely. "You and your Adam and Eve! I'm a Communist, that's what I am. Communist or Anarchist, it all comes to much the same thing." And he went round the house, muttering when the fit took him: "Adam and Eve! Adam and Eve! Nothing better to do with their time than pick bleeding apples!"

III

I don't know how we got through that day, but I was very glad when it was over, the tea things were cleared away, and Belcher said in his peaceable way: "Well, chums, what about it?" We sat round the table and Hawkins took out the cards, and just then I heard Jeremiah Donovan's footsteps on the path and a dark presentiment crossed my mind. I rose from the table and caught him before he reached the door.

"What do you want?" I asked.

"I want those two soldier friends of yours," he said, getting red.

"Is that the way, Jeremiah Donovan?" I asked.

"That's the way. There were four of our lads shot this morning, one of them a boy of sixteen."

"That's bad," I said.

At that moment Noble followed me out, and the three of us walked down the path together, talking in whispers. Feeney, the local intelligence officer, was standing by the gate.

"What are you going to do about it?" I asked Jeremiah Donovan.

"I want you and Noble to get them out; tell them they're being shifted again; that'll be the quietest way."

"Leave me out of that," said Noble, under his breath.

Jeremiah Donovan looked at him hard.

"All right," he says. "You and Feeney get a few tools from the shed and dig a hole by the far end of the bog. Bonaparte and myself will be after you. Don't let anyone see you with the tools. I wouldn't like it to go beyond ourselves."

We saw Feeney and Noble go round to the shed and went in ourselves. I left Jeremiah Donovan to do the explanations. He told them that he had orders to send them back to the Second Battalion. Hawkins let out a mouthful of curses, and you could see that though Belcher didn't say anything, he was a bit upset too. The old woman was for having them stay in spite of us, and she didn't stop advising them until Jeremiah Donovan lost his temper and turned on her. He had a nasty temper, I noticed. It was pitch dark in the cottage by this time, but no one thought of lighting the lamp, and in the darkness the two Englishmen fetched their topcoats and said good-bye to the old woman.

"Just as a man makes a home of a bleeding place, some bastard at headquarters thinks you're too cushy and shunts you off," said Hawkins, shaking her hand.

"A thousand thanks, madam," said Belcher. "A thousand thanks for everything" – as though he'd made it up.

We went round to the back of the house and down towards the bog. It was only then that Jeremiah Donovan told them. He was shaking with excitement.

"There were four of our fellows shot in Cork this morning and now you are to be shot as a reprisal."

"What are you talking about?" snaps Hawkins. "It's bad enough being mucked about as we are without having to put up with your funny jokes."

"It isn't a joke," said Donovan. "I'm sorry, Hawkins, but it's true," and begins on the usual rigmarole about duty and how unpleasant it is. I never noticed that people who talk a lot about duty find it much of a trouble to them.

"Oh, cut it out!" said Hawkins.

"Ask Bonaparte," said Donovan, seeing that Hawkins wasn't taking him seriously. "Isn't it true, Bonaparte?"

"It is," I said, and Hawkins stopped.

"Ah, for Christ's sake, chum!"

"I mean it, chum," I said.

"You don't sound as if you meant it."

"If he doesn't mean it, I do," said Donovan, working himself up.

"What have you against me, Jeremiah Donovan?"

"I never said I had anything against you. But why did your people take out four of your prisoners and shoot them in cold blood?"

He took Hawkins by the arm and dragged him on, but it was impossible to make him understand that we were in earnest. I had the Smith and Wesson in my pocket and I kept fingering it and wondering what I'd do if they put up a fight for it or ran, and wishing to God they'd do one or the other. I knew if they did run for it, that I'd never fire on them. Hawkins wanted to know was Noble in it, and when we said yes, he asked us why Noble wanted to plug him. Why did any of us want to plug him? What had he done to us? Weren't we all chums? Didn't we understand him and didn't he understand us? Did we imagine for an instant that he'd shoot us for all the so-and-so officers in the so-and-so British Army?

By this time we'd reached the bog, and I was so sick I couldn't even answer him. We walked along the edge of it in the darkness, and every now and then Hawkins would call a halt and begin all over again, as if he was wound up, about our being chums, and I knew that nothing but the sight of the grave would convince him that we had to do it. And all the time I was hoping that something would happen; that they'd run for it or that Noble would take over the responsibility from me. I had the feeling that it was worse on Noble than on me.

IV

At last we saw the lantern in the distance and made towards it. Noble was carrying it, and Feeney was standing somewhere in the darkness behind him, and the picture of them so still and silent in the bogland brought it home to me that we were in earnest, and banished the last bit of hope I had.

Belcher, on recognising Noble, said: "Hallo, chum," in his quiet way, but Hawkins flew at him at once, and the argument began all over again, only this time Noble had nothing to say for himself and stood with his head down, holding the lantern between his legs.

It was Jeremiah Donovan who did the answering. For the twentieth time, as though it was haunting his mind, Hawkins asked if anybody thought he'd shoot Noble.

"Yes, you would," said Jeremiah Donovan.

"No, I wouldn't, damn you!"

"You would, because you'd know you'd be shot for not doing it."

"I wouldn't, not if I was to be shot twenty times over. I wouldn't shoot a pal. And Belcher wouldn't – isn't that right, Belcher?"

"That's right, chum," Belcher said, but more by way of answering the question than of joining in the argument. Belcher sounded as though whatever unforeseen thing he'd always been waiting for had come at last.

"Anyway, who says Noble would be shot if I wasn't? What do you think I'd do if I was in his place, out in the middle of a blasted bog?"

"What would you do?" asked Donovan.

"I'd go with him wherever he was going, of course. Share my last bob with him and stick by him through thick and thin. No one can ever say of me that I let down a pal."

"We've had enough of this," said Jeremiah Donovan, cocking his revolver. "Is there any message you want to send?"

"No, there isn't."

"Do you want to say your prayers?"

Hawkins came out with a cold-blooded remark that even shocked me and turned on Noble again.

"Listen to me Noble," he said. "You and me are chums. You can't come over to my side, so I'll come over to your side. That show you I mean what I say? Give me a rifle and I'll go along with you and the other lads."

Noble answered him. We knew that was no way out.

"Hear what I'm saying?" he said. "I'm through with it. I'm a deserter or anything else you like. I don't believe in your stuff, but it's no worse than mine. That satisfy you?"

Noble raised his head, but Donovan began to speak and he lowered it again without replying.

"For the last time, have you any messages to send?" said Donovan in a cold, excited sort of voice.

"Shut up, Donovan! You don't understand me, but these lads do. They're not the sort to make a pal and kill a pal. They're not the tools of any capitalist."

I alone of the crowd saw Donovan raise his Webley to the back of Hawkins's neck, and as he did so I shut my eyes and tried to pray. Hawkins had begun to say something else when Donovan fired, and as I opened my eyes at the bang, I saw Hawkins stagger at the knees and lie out flat at Noble's feet, slowly and as quiet as a kid falling asleep, with the lanternlight on his lean legs and bright farmer's boots. We all stood very still, watching him settle out in the last agony.

Then Belcher took out a handkerchief and began to tie it about his own eyes (in our excitement we'd forgotten to do the same for Hawkins), and, seeing it wasn't big enough, turned and asked for the loan of mine. I gave it to him, and he knotted the two together and pointed with his foot at Hawkins.

"He's not quite dead," he said. "Better give him another."

Sure enough, Hawkins's left knee was beginning to rise. I bent down and put my gun to his head; then recollecting myself, I got up again. Belcher understood what was in my mind.

"Give him his first," he said. "I don't mind. Poor bastard, we don't know what's happening to him now."

I knelt and fired. By this time I didn't seem to know what I was doing. Belcher, who was fumbling a bit awkwardly with the handkerchiefs, came out with a laugh as he heard the shot. It was the first time I had heard him laugh and it sent a shudder down my back; it sounded so unnatural.

"Poor bugger!" he said quietly. "And last night he was so curious about it all. It's very queer, chums, I always think. Now he knows as much about it as they'll ever let him know, and last night he was all in the dark."

Donovan helped him to tie the handkerchiefs about his eyes. "Thanks, chum," he said. Donovan asked if there were any messages he wanted sent.

"No, chum," he said. "Not for me. If any of you would like to write to Hawkins's mother, you'll find a letter from her in his pocket. He and his mother were great chums. But my missus left me eight years ago. Went away with another fellow and took the kid with her. I like the feeling of a home, as you may have noticed, but I couldn't start another again after that."

It was an extraordinary thing, but in those few minutes Belcher said more than in all the weeks before. It was just as if the sound of the shot had started a flood of talk in him and he could go on the whole night like that, quite happily, talking about himself. We stood around like fools now that he couldn't see us any longer. Donovan looked at Noble, and Noble shook his head. Then Donovan raised his Webley, and at that moment Belcher gave his queer laugh again. He may have thought we were talking about him, or perhaps he noticed the same thing I'd noticed and couldn't understand it.

"Excuse me, chums," he said. "I feel I'm talking the hell of a lot, and so silly, about my being so handy about a house and things like that. But this thing came on me suddenly. You'll forgive me, I'm sure."

"You don't want to say a prayer?" asked Donovan.

"No, chum," he said. "I don't think it would help. I'm ready, and you boys want to get it over."

"You understand that we're only doing our duty," said Donovan.

Belcher's head was raised like a blind man's, so that you could only see his chin and the top of his nose in the lantern-light.

"I never could make out what duty was myself," he said. "I think you're all good lads, if that's what you mean. I'm not complaining."

Noble, just as if he couldn't bear any more of it, raised his fist at Donovan, and in a flash Donovan raised his gun and fired. The big man went over like a sack of meal, and this time there was no need for a second shot.

I don't remember much about the burying, but that it was worse than all the rest because we had to carry them to the grave. It was all mad lonely with nothing but a patch of lantern-light between ourselves and the dark, and birds hooting and screeching all round, disturbed by the guns. Noble went through Hawkins's belongings to find the letter from his mother, and then joined his hands together. He did the same with Belcher. Then, when we'd filled in the grave, we separated from Jeremiah Donovan and Feeney and took our tools back to the shed. All the way we didn't speak a word. The kitchen was dark and cold as we'd left it, and the old woman was sitting over the hearth, saying her beads. We walked past her into the room, and Noble struck a match to light the lamp. She rose quietly and came to the doorway with all her cantankerousness gone.

"What did ye do with them?" she asked in a whisper, and Noble started so that the match went out in his hand.

"What's that?" he asked without turning round.

"I heard ye," she said.

"What did you hear?" asked Noble.

"I heard ye. Do you think I didn't hear ye, putting the spade back in the houseen?"

Noble struck another match and this time the lamp lit for him.

"Was that what ye did to them?" she asked.

Then, by God, in the very doorway, she fell on her knees and began praying, and after looking at her for a minute or two Noble did the same by the fireplace. I pushed my way out past her and left them at it. I stood at the door, watching the stars and listening to the shrieking of the birds dying out over the bogs. It is so strange what you feel at times like that that you can't describe it. Noble says he saw everything ten times the size, as though there were nothing in the whole world but that little patch of bog with the two Englishmen stiffening into it, but with me it was as if the patch of bog where the Englishmen were was a million miles away, and even Noble and the old woman, mumbling behind me, and the birds and the bloody stars were all far away, and I was somehow very small and very lost and lonely like a child astray in the snow. And anything that happened to me afterwards, I never felt the same about again.

Biographical Notes

Frank O'Connor (pseudonym of Michael O'Donovan) is probably the most popular of Irish short story writers. He was born in Cork City in 1903. Though he received only a minimum of formal schooling (his family being very poor), he developed an interest in literature and languages at a very early age, and picked up considerable knowledge from various sources. He earned his living for a while from a series of odd jobs as a teacher of French, German and Irish. His interest in Irish (the language of his West Cork grandmother) was to a large extent inspired by the Irish cultural revival which had gathered strength in his youth. He soon became an expert on Gaelic literature, and published a number of translations into English.

Though he joined the Irish Volunteers (later I.R.A.) as a teenager, he was too young to take an active part in the struggle for national independence. He did, however, fight in the Civil War (1920–1922) on the Republican side, against those who wanted to accept the compromise of the 1920 Treaty. He was becoming increasingly disillusioned with the consequences of blind faith in abstract ideals when the war ended and he spent a year in prison camps. Such experiences provided him with the material for his first collection of stories, Guests of the Nation *(1931): he is represented here by its title story.*

With his growing success as a writer, he became a part of the literary establishment in the early years of the Irish Free State (later Republic). However, he soon came in conflict with its censorship laws, and a number of his works – including even some translations from the Gaelic – were banned for their alleged indecency. In the 1950s he moved to the United States, where he taught at Harvard and Stanford Universities.

In spite of such conflicts with officialdom, there is little trace of bitterness in even his latest stories. In his treatment of Irish life, humour prevails, as well as sympathy and respect for the autonomy of his characters. After suffering a stroke in 1961 he returned to Ireland, and continued to write for a number of years. His last work was a critical study of the literary form he had excelled in, called The Lonely Voice. *He died in Dublin in 1966.*

Annotations

14 1 **to shift** to move – 2 **chum** *Engl. sl.* friend – 5 **Jeremiah** [ˌdʒerəˈmaɪə] – 7 **divil** *Ir. dial.* devil – 8 **the trey** the three (in a card game) – 10 **to be a fair hand at s.th.** to be good at s.th. – 12 **gaiters** protective coverings worn over trouser-legs – **pants** *Ir.* and *Am.* trousers – 13 **to tilt** to bend over to one side – 15 **broad accent** strong dialect pronunciation – 19 **from this to Claregalway** [ˌkleə(r)ˈgɒlweɪ] (a village in County Galway) idiomatic phrase meaning 'just about anywhere' – 20 **to take to s.th.** to get used to, to become a part of s.th. – 26 **bloke** *Engl. sl.* fellow, man – 30 **decent chaps** pleasant, likeable young men – 31 **The Walls of Limerick ... Waves of Tory** Irish reels danced in groups

15 7 **accents you could cut with a knife** strong (English) accents – **khaki tunics** light brown jackets (worn in combination with black trousers by members of the notorious "Black and Tans" – an auxiliary force recruited to help the British Army suppress the Irish rebels, 1918–21) – 11 **a great warrant to** *Ir. coll.* very good at, very fond of – **cranky** bad-tempered – 19 **turf** *Ir.* peat, used in Ireland for burning in open fires – 24 **platoon** an organized group of soldiers – 27 **to skin s.o.** *sl.* to take all a person's money and belongings – 30 **gab** *Ir. coll.* talk – 37 **a fright to** *Ir. coll.* very good at, and fond of (doing s.th. annoying) – 38 **to get stuck in** *Ir. coll.* to get involved in an argument with – 39 **his match** his equal – 40 **drought** [aʊ] dry period, lack of rain

16 1 **deity** [ˈdiːətɪ] god – 4 **to pucker** to draw together in folds – 5 **crab's mouth** *here:* small, with a hard expression – 8 **divinity** god – 20 **to lose one's temper** to get angry – 23 **sneer** expression of contempt – 25 **Jehoshophat** [–ˈ–––] – 29 **bleeding** *vulg. sl.* meaningless swear word, like 'bloody'

17 4 **hostage** person held captive until certain demands are met – 10 **unforeseen** *here:* unthinking – 19 **vet** *coll.* veterinary surgeon (who sometimes has to kill old or ailing animals) – 30 **saucy** cheeky, impertinent – 33 **sweet damn-all** *sl.* nothing – 39 **chit** *sl.* piece of paper to show one is entitled to s.th.

18 8 **to plug** *here:* to shoot – 9 **to put the wind up** *coll.* to make nervous or afraid – 26 **presentiment** a feeling about the future – 30 **Is that the way?** *Ir. dial.* (transl. from Gaelic) Is that so? – 35 **intelligence officer** spy

19 6 **bog** area of land covered with turf (peat) – 20 **cushy** [ʊ] *coll.* comfortable – **to shunt** to move s.o. or s.th. backwards and forwards (like a train) – 28 **as a reprisal** (military usage) in revenge – 30 **to be mucked about** to be pushed around – 32 **rigmarole** long story or explanation – 35 **cut it out** *coll.* stop talking nonsense

20 7 **Smith and Wesson** kind of pistol – 15 **so-and-so** *here:* stands for some unprintable words actually used – 19 **wound up** (like a clock or clockwork toy) – 27 **to banish** to send away – 33 **to haunt** to be constantly present in

21 2 **pal** *coll.* friend – 7 **blasted** *here:* meaningless swear word – 9 **bob** *coll.* shilling (= 5p in the new currency) – 12 **to cock a revolver** to raise a lever in preparation for firing – 32 **Webley** kind of pistol – 35 **to stagger** to lose one's balance, to move unsteadily – 38 **agony** great pain

22 1 **asked for the loan** asked to borrow – 12 **shudder** shiver – 13 **bugger** *vulg. sl., here:* expression of sympathy – 20 **missus** *sl.* wife

23 5 **meal** corn for feeding animals – 7 **mad lonely** very lonely – 15 **saying her beads** saying the rosary – 17 **cantankerousness** bad-temperedness – 18 **ye** *Ir. dial.* plural of 'you' – 24 **houseen** *Ir. dial.* little house (from *Gael.* '-ín', diminutive ending) – 30 **shrieking** shrill crying – 36 **bloody** *sl., here:* habitual use of a swear-word to express any feeling – 38 **astray** lost

Interpretation and Teaching Notes

Background, Content and Analysis

As indicated in the Biographical Notes, the background of "Guests of the Nation" is the author's experience of the struggle for Irish independence and the subsequent Civil War. In a sense, this story could be said to sum up his personal development in those years, or at least to crystallize the conflicting tendencies of idealism and realism, enthusiasm and detachment in the young revolutionary and writer.

One incident described in *An Only Child* (the first volume of Frank O'Connor's two-part autobiography) casts considerable light on the feelings that went into the writing of this story. Caught up in the euphoria of the Gaelic Revival and the nationalist movement, and strongly influenced by his teacher, the writer and patriot Daniel Corkery, he had taken the radical side in the post-Treaty split in the movement. This was also the side taken by one of the leading figures of the rebellion, Erskine Childers, who – incongruously – was an Englishman. In his book, O'Connor describes how he and his comrades tried to save Childers from capture by the Free State troops; but he finally fell into their hands and was executed:

> ... again and again in my own imagination, I have had to go through those last few terrible moments with him almost as though I were there: see the slight figure of the little grey-haired Englishman emerge for the last time into the Irish daylight, apparently cheerful and confident but incapable of grandiose gestures, concerned only lest inadvertently he might do or say something that would distress some fool of an Irish boy who was about to level an English rifle at his heart.[1]

The incident which makes up the action of "Guests of the Nation" is set in a period in which the issues were somewhat more clear-cut, but the same sense of the absurdity of it all is there.

The story is told from the point of view of a young revolutionary with the fanciful nickname of Bonaparte. The first-person narrative establishes a closeness between author, protagonist/narrator and reader, the development of which is an important element in the structure of the story. In Part I, the identification is almost complete: we share Bonaparte's naive pleasure in the cosy companionship that develops between the group of I.R.A.

1 Frank O'Connor, *An Only Child*, p. 238

men and their "guests", the two Englishmen, Belcher and Hawkins. But in spite of the card-playing, the dances, and the gleeful adoption by Bonaparte and his friend Noble of the men's "curious" English slang, there are frequent reminders that the idyllic calm is illusory – or, seen from another point of view, that it represents an island of sanity in the surrounding madness.

It soon becomes clear that the "guests" are actually prisoners, though Bonaparte cannot see the sense in guarding them, as they show no signs of wanting to escape (p. 14, ll. 17–21; p. 15, ll. 4–9). A hint of the ideological background of the war they are involved in is given in the form of a remark to the effect that, though the Irish boys could teach Hawkins to dance 'The Walls of Limerick', they themselves "did not dance foreign dances on principle". The oblique reference to the Englishmen's clothes is also an indication that the Englishmen are members of the notorious 'Black-and-Tans', an auxiliary force recruited specially for the purpose of putting down the rebellion, and responsible for numerous atrocities. This fact does not seem to bother the I.R.A. men, however, who obviously perceive Belcher and Hawkins as fellow human beings, and not as wearers of a uniform.

Part II sees Jeremiah Donovan emerge as a key figure in the story. Whereas he had been introduced as a simple peasant and something of a figure of fun for the more 'sophisticated' town-dwellers Noble and Bonaparte, it now turns out that it is he who insists on upholding the logic of the war they are involved in against the claims of friendship. He seems, furthermore, to be totally unaffected by the spirit of comradeship that has developed between captors and prisoners (p. 16, ll. 13–14). His revelation (p. 17, ll. 3–4) that the Englishmen are being held as hostages comes as something of a shock to both reader and narrator. The irony implicit in the two scenes which follow, with Hawkins sounding off as usual on his disbelief in God and a next world (p. 17, l. 26 – p 18 l. 21), is something we can presume Bonaparte also perceives, and we share his discomfiture.

The next section starts, as the first section had, with Belcher suggesting a game of cards – but now the situation is completely different. The tension rises considerably with the news – not yet conveyed to the Englishmen – that four Irish prisoners have been shot by the British in Cork. When told that they are to be moved to another battalion, the Englishmen's reaction is to complain about the loss of the "home" (p. 19, l. 19) they had found in the old woman's farmhouse. When finally told that they are to be shot, it is Bonaparte's attitude that is of greatest interest: whatever his private feelings, he continues to identify with the group he belongs to – and with Jeremiah Donovan. He may wish the two would escape (p. 20, ll. 8–10), but he nevertheless states that "we were in earnest" (l. 7) and "we had to do it" (l. 20). At this point most readers will have parted company with him as a figure of identification, though one can still sympathize with him in his dilemma.

The final section (Part IV) is devoted to the reactions of the various characters in the face of the actual shooting of the Englishmen. With Donovan representing inhuman fanaticism, Noble and Bonaparte either passive or subjected to ideas of patriotic duty, and the old woman out of sight, the only characters that retain our full sympathies are the two Englishmen. Hawkins remains true to to himself right up to the end. There is no let-up in his stream of obscenities, but his arguments are plausible (one can see no good reason why the I.R.A. men cannot accept his offer to desert and fight on their side), and his plea for the primacy of friendship unassailable. Belcher begins to talk and reveals something of what was previously hidden under his quiet exterior, and which explains his gratitude for the feeling of 'home' he had found with the group in the old farmhouse: a loneliness and despair which enables him to face death with equanimity. It is Donovan who does the actual shooting, due to the scruples of the others. However, when the first shot fails to kill Hawkins outright, it is Bonaparte who finishes him off (p. 22, ll. 4–9). Whatever his excuses, he must now live with the knowledge that he has killed a friend.

The traumatic nature of the experience for him is hinted at in his remark that he "didn't seem to know what [he] was doing", and in his dazed account of the burying of the Englishmen (p. 23, ll. 6–13). His shock thus brings him close to the level of consciousness already reached by the reader, and this effects a partial reconciliation with him. When Noble and the old woman seek consolation in prayer, Bonaparte walks out past them, leaving them at it, as he says (ll. 27–29); this suggests a rejection of the simple solution in favour of acceptance of the full burden of guilt – though such philosophic considerations would be beyond the scope of the young man's mind in the circumstances. What comes across most clearly in the last paragraph is the young man groping for words to express the desolateness he feels in a world in which all the values he had lived by are distorted by the rigid application of abstract ideas such as 'duty'. The lack of human warmth is combined with total (moral) disorientation in the image of the "child astray in the snow".

Though the moral standpoint of the author in relation to the events portrayed in this story is clearly expressed through its overall structure (which could be characterized as one of growing alienation from the representatives of inhuman devotion to duty), it is interesting to note the connotations of the names he chose for his characters[2]. Since the narrator comes closest to a portrayal of the author in his youth, naming him 'Bonaparte' could be an ironic comment on his and his comrades' youthful romantic delusions – the same holds true for 'Noble'. On the other hand, he gave his villain his own real name, which suggests a complicity between the naive idealism of people like himself and the brutality and inhumanity of the actual war. Donovan's name also links him with the theorists of the revolution – one of the most revered of 19th century nationalist heroes carried the name of Jeremiah O'Donovan Rossa. The obvious implication is that no one involved in the revolutionary movement is completely innocent of responsibility for its excesses.

2 Cf. Earl F. Briden, "Guests of the Nation: A Final Irony"

First Unit
The Characters, the Setting and the Unfolding of the Situation

Preparation: The students should have read at least parts I and II.

1. The first paragraph
Right at the beginning of the story you are introduced to a number of different characters. How much do you learn about them in the eight lines which make up the first paragraph?
Five characters mentioned; some of their physical characteristics; their division into two groups:
"they" – the two Englishmen, Belcher (big) and Hawkins (small);
"we" – Noble, narrator (as yet nameless) and Jeremiah Donovan.
But the characters behave "as if" (l. 7) there were no such division.

2. Characterization in part I
What have you learned about the characters by the end of part I?
"Noble and myself" are described as "young" (p. 14, l. 23).
Noble: pious but not good at arguing religion (p. 15, ll. 31–34).
Narrator: nickname 'Bonaparte' (p. 14, l. 26), seems to take a childish delight in the goings-on around him (p. 15, ll. 10–11).
Jeremiah Donovan is described as a simple countryman, shy, sober, slow, but reliable in dealing with documents (p.14, ll. 9–16).

Belcher: a big man, very silent, good at cards, very polite to the old lady (p. 14, ll. 1, 9–10; p. 15, ll. 10–23).
Hawkins: small, talkative, argumentative, strongly anti-religious, uses a lot of bad language (p. 14, ll. 5–7; p. 15, ll. 23–38).
Both of the Englismen are described as adapting well to their new surroundings (p. 14, ll. 18–21, 25, 32; p. 15, ll. 4–5, etc.).
Extra character, introduced on page 15 – the old woman, a bit eccentric, and well the match of Hawkins in argument (p. 15, l. 39 – p. 16, l. 11).

3. The geographical and historical setting
How does it become clear where and in what historical situation the story is set? (Pay particular attention to the passage from p. 14, l. 17 to p. 15, l. 12.)
First paragraph: a country where Englishmen are foreigners;
Third paragraph: it becomes clear that the Englishmen are prisoners (l. 17). The reference to the "Second Battalion" (l. 22) indicates that a war or rebellion is going on; the details given on p. 15, ll. 1–8 – refusal to dance foreign dances, khaki tunics, etc. – makes it clear which: the Irish fight for Independence, 1918–20. A group of I.R.A. men are holding two Englishmen (members of the notorious 'Black-and-Tans') prisoner in a farmhouse occupied by an old woman somewhere in the country.

4. The unfolding of the situation
What new information is provided about the characters in part II? What effect does it have?
In most cases, just confirmation of what we have already learned: Noble's naivety, Hawkins' anti-clericalism, etc. But we share the narrator's surprise at Donovan's lack of love for the two Englishmen. This paves the way for the explicit information (p. 17, ll. 3–7) on their real situation: the "guests" (p. 15, l. 12) have now turned into "hostages" (p. 17, l. 4).

Homework: Read the story to the end, to find out what happens, and how it affects those involved.

Second Unit
Structure and Meaning

Note: This Unit contains enough material for two consecutive lessons. If such a double period is not available, it is recommended that the material be reduced to points 2, 3, 4 and 5, with the diagram introduced at an earlier point.

1. Time scheme

How much time is covered by the action of our story, and how is this time divided among the four parts? – What else distinguishes the four parts?

About 24 hours;	[Part I: previous events]	–	Exposition (cf. First Unit)
	Part II: one evening	–	beginning of action
	Part III: next day	–	crisis, turning point
	Part IV: second evening	–	conclusion, denouement

The time scheme, however, gives only a very rough idea of how the story develops. The four parts also differ in tension and mood.

2. Function of parts I and II in the whole scheme of things

Now that you know how the story ends, what would you say is the function

– of the friendly scenes of part I?

– and of the information provided in part II?

The early scenes establish an atmosphere of friendship, trust and humanity, which makes the actual outcome of the story seem all the more grotesque. What we learn in part II reminds us that the two groups are enemies, and that the logic of war may take precedence over the logic of friendship. This builds up considerable tension.

3. Point of view as a structural element in parts I and II

How (by what principle) does the author organize the gradual build-up of tension?

We see everything through Bonaparte's eyes; by sharing in his limited viewpoint, we also share his gradual realization of the real situation, and can identify with his feelings up to a point (esp. p. 19, ll. 11–12).

4. Effect of point of view in parts III and IV

Describe Bonaparte's feelings up to the time they actually lead their prisoners out into the bog (end of part III).

Seems to be in a state of shock and confusion (p. 18, l. 22); wishes the two Englishmen would escape (p. 20, ll. 7–10); but he still regards himself as being on the same side as Jeremiah Donovan, and sees no other alternative but that "we had to do it" (l. 20).

Did you find yourself agreeing or disagreeing with Bonaparte, that they "had to do it"? Give reasons.

Individual answers and discussion. Points to be considered: Could the two young men have encouraged the Englishmen to escape? Could they have openly mutinied against Jeremiah Donovan? Why didn't they accept Hawkins' suggestion (p. 21, ll. 18–24)? What is Bonaparte's attitude to the shooting of the Irish prisoners in Cork (p. 17, ll. 15–20; p. 18, ll. 31–33)?

Most likely conclusion: There were alternatives, but Bonaparte finally subjects himself – however unwillingly – to the 'logic' of patriotic duty.
How does this affect your attitude to Bonaparte?
We may still sympathize with him in his dilemma, but we no longer naively identify with him. Our full sympathies now remain with the Englishmen.

5. The other characters' development
How do the Englishmen and the other characters behave under the influence of the situation? Do they change or remain the same?
Hawkins remains true to himself right up to the end – continues to curse and swear, but his arguments are plausible, and his plea for his friends to behave like friends fully understandable.
Belcher reveals hidden depths of character; resignation; begins to talk and reveals his loneliness and despair – we now understand his previous silence and reserve.
Noble – reactions similar to Bonaparte; tries to hit Donovan when it is too late to change anything; looks for comfort in prayer at the end.
Donovan remains the same all through – no change since he was revealed to be unscrupulous and lacking in human feelings.

6. Patterns of alienation in the story as a whole
Taking Jeremiah Donovan as representative of 'duty' and inhumanity, we can represent Bonaparte's – and the reader's – changing attitude to him in a diagram. [This should be constructed stage by stage on the blackboard, or by the gradual addition of transparencies on the OH-projector. The key passages are: p. 14, ll. 5–16; p. 16, ll. 13–15; p. 17, ll. 1–26; p. 19, ll. –18; p. 20, ll. 6–20; p. 22, ll. 3–9; p. 23, ll. 6–39.]

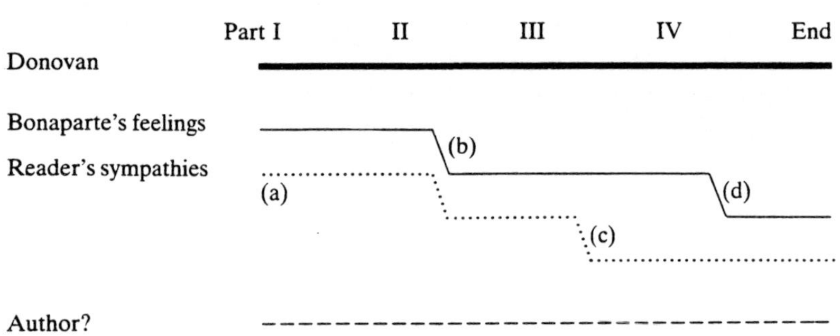

a) Illusion of harmony
b) Revelation about Jeremiah Donovan – loses sympathy of Bonaparte and reader.
c) Bonaparte's acceptance of 'duty' – reader ceases to identify with him.
d) Bonaparte's trauma – his realization that, whatever his excuses, he has killed his friend; his shock brings him close to the level of consciousness already reached by the reader – partial reconciliation.

7. Meaning as revealed in structure
Where do you think the author's sympathies are?
The way the author tells the story (i.e. its structure) is the most reliable guide to his intentions in writing it, i.e. to its overall meaning. The basic structure is one of growing distance from the representatives of 'man's inhumanity to man' and abstract ideas such as 'duty'. This entitles us to say that this is an 'anti-war' story.

Homework: Re-read the story, paying special attention to the way the various characters speak. Pick out all deviations from 'standard English'.

Third Unit
Language as a Vehicle of Characterization and Social Context

1. Language of the narrative and its effect
How would you describe the language of the narrative, i.e. the 'tone of voice' in which Bonaparte relates the events he experienced? Take as an example the passage on page 14, lines 17–21, and the last paragraph.
Informal, colloquial, uses colourful idioms, occasional short forms; sounds like natural speaking voice, as if chatting with friends.
This is also true of the last paragraph, but the images are more poetic. Here, we still get the impression of spontaneous speech, with Bonaparte groping for words to express what he feels. Effect: credibility, sympathy; the desolateness of the "child astray in the snow" comes across all the more strongly.

2. Deviations from 'standard English'
Compare the language used by Bonaparte (e.g. page 15, ll. 27–38) with that used by Hawkins. How significant are the similarities and differences? (Use your Annotations.)
Both use a lot of colloquialisms and slang expressions – the similarity makes it easy for them to understand each other and become friends. The collo-

quial expressions used by Bonaparte are mainly 'Irishisms'. Hawkins' language consists mainly of English slang, often vulgar – characterization as working-class Englishman. The importance of the English-Irish difference is hinted at at the beginning of the story (p. 14, ll. 3–4).

3. Language differences within the Irish group
Examine the way the Irish characters speak. Consider differences we are told about explicitly, and those you can detect yourself.
Noble and Bonaparte laugh at Donovan's country accent (p. 14, ll. 15–16, example ll. 7–8); the difference is not very great, however (cf. p. 19, ll. 30–31) – whether country or town, they share a similar cultural background. The old woman's use of dialect forms based on the Irish language (p. 23, ll. 20–26) remind us that she belongs to a generation that is closer to the original Gaelic culture.

4. Study of 'A Note on the Language', p. 4/6. [If the O'Flaherty story is to be read immediately after this, indicate that the setting is a geographically and culturally more remote area of Ireland, where the Irish language is still spoken.] .

For Further Study

Points for discussion

1. What significance can you find in the names the author gave to his characters?
2. Study the way the characters differ in their attitude to religion.

Courses/Projects based on this story

1. Stories by Frank O'Connor
"Guests of the Nation" plus at least three of the following (available in *The Stories of Frank O'Connor*, London 1953, and various paperback editions):
- "First Confession"
- "My Oedipus Complex" – also included in *Humorous Short Stories* (Langenscheidt) and *Growing Up* (Hirschgraben)
- "The Procession of Life" – from *Guests of the Nation* (Poolbeg paperback, Dublin)
- "Peasants" – included in *Irish Short Stories* (Schöningh)

- "The Majesty of the Law" – included in *Contemporary British Short Stories I* (CVK) and *The Man of the House and Other Stories* (Aschendorff)
- "Judas" – included in *The Man of the House and Other Stories* (Aschendorff)

2. Political Violence in Irish Short Stories

- Frank O'Connor: "Guests of the Nation"
- Michael McLaverty: "Pigeons" – extract included in Topical Texts 19: *Youth – Problems and Challenge* (Klett)
- Liam O'Flaherty: "The Sniper" – included in *Contemporary British Short Stories* (Hueber); simplified version in *Learning English, Compact Course 4* (Klett)
- Mary Lavin: "The Patriot Son" – simplified version in *One True Friend and Other Irish Short Stories* (Longman-Langenscheidt)

Liam O'Flaherty

A Red Petticoat

Mrs Mary Deignan and her four children were sitting around the fire in their cabin. They were very miserable. For the reason that the day was a cold one in the middle of February, and there was no food in the house. That morning they ate the last piece of oaten cake, and there was no more oats to make another cake. Their flour had given out a week before that. A dried fish that Coleman, the eldest child and the only son, had stolen off a wall where it was getting dried after being taken out of pickle, had lasted them three days for dinner. There was not a single scrap in the house. Not even a piece of potato.

"Well," said the mother, "what are we doing here? We must do something. God is good, no doubt, but he is good only to those who forage for themselves. Now what's to be done? Children, can none of you think of anything? Isn't it well known that the angels put wisdom into the mouths of little ones? Though, God forgive me, the four little ones I have are bigger than myself, at least as far as their stomachs are concerned. So they are."

The four children, in spite of their hunger and their misery, began to laugh. They were really a remarkable family. The mother was remarkable and the children were remarkable. Since the father, old Mick Deignan, that had the wart on his nose, and was always sick with the influenza, and always wore a white frieze trousers that somehow or other always had a yellow burnt spot on its leg one place or another, since he died ten years before that the family had been very, very poor. They had ten acres of land, but they had no stock to put on it, so they always rented it for a few pounds a year. The mother worked at any odd job that she could find, washing, thickening frieze, and scrubbing in people's houses, and the daughters used to mend nets for the co-operative society, while the son, who was seventeen years of age, worked as a labourer. But, to tell the truth, as far as work was concerned, they were a lazy and indigent family. Maybe they would work well enough for a spell, and then for some reason or other the whole family took to idleness and sat in their cabin all day composing poems, cracking jokes, drinking tea, and having the time of their lives. So that the villagers, passing their cabin and hearing loud laughter, got mad with rage against these poor devils who were gifted by the good God who governs all things with the Divine capacity for enjoying life and their good health. For in spite of their cabin containing only one tiny bedroom where the mother and her three daughters slept, and the little kitchen where the son slept on the settle, the children were healthy. And the mother was healthy, except in cold weather when she drank too much tea and suffered so terribly from flatulence and pains all over her middle, that she was always on the point of death and moaned like a possessed one.

But that winter things had gone badly with them until now they were at the end of their tether. Their credit was exhausted. Their solitary pig had been taken from the sty in lieu of debt by Flanagan, the grocer from Kilmurrage, "the curse of God on his rotten Co. Mayo liver", as Mrs Deignan said. None of them could find work anywhere. Until now they had bravely kept up courage and laughed and sang and composed poems, satires on all their enemies, but the hunger was telling on them that bitterly cold day as they sat by the fire. Barbara, the eldest daughter, aged sixteen, was trying to toast her short, fat legs at the turf fire.

She was sitting on a low stool in the corner, her short, thick black hair woven in a plait that hung over her shoulders. Her soft, open red lips and her big, black eyes were turned towards her legs that were bare to the knees, and her short, stubby little hands were moving up and down the legs, counting the "rockfishes" on them, that is the queer blue spots that came into them from being constantly exposed in their nakedness to the turf blaze. Mary, aged fifteen, a girl almost exactly similar in shape and face to Barbara, except that she was slightly thinner, had her left leg in her lap and with her two hands she was pulling at the big toe. She had an idea that if she pulled at her toes long enough she could make them as long and slender as her fingers and thus be a great lady. Little Margaret, the most serious of the family, aged fourteen, the one who always discovered the correct phrase when the rest of the family were in a difficulty over a poem, sat very seriously with her little hands folded in her lap, looking at the fire, with her black curls hanging about her little pale face. Coleman, a handsome boy of seventeen, with large blue eyes and long lashes like a woman, lay stretched on the form beside his mother, looking at the fire and brooding over something. He was always thinking and breathing heavily through his nose, and then all of a sudden he would slap his thigh and jump to his feet bursting with laughter, and no matter how much people asked him what he was laughing at and what had come into his head, he would just shake his shoulders and say nothing.

The mother sat in the other corner opposite Barbara. She was about sixty and very thin and old-looking on account of the yellowish colour of her wrinkled face, a colour she got very presumably from her tea drinking and her bad digestion. When she had her clothes on and she was talking she looked big enough, but when she stripped going to bed she was so thin and small that it was a continual cause of wonder to Margaret that she didn't break in the middle. They called her "Mary of the Bad Verses" in the village and all over the whole island of Inverara, not because her verses were bad as verses, but because they were scurrilous and abusive, and at times even indecent and in a sense immoral.

"Well," said the mother, again, "have you got any plans, Coleman?"

Coleman looked at his mother seriously with his big eyelashes drooping and his round, red mouth half open. Then he giggled and nestled farther down on the form like a child that is playing with its mother.

"If there are any plans to be made," he said, still giggling, "you'd better make them yourself. I'm too hungry to think about anything."

"Yes, mother, think of something," cried the other three children, suddenly becoming excited.

"Well," said the mother, setting herself squat on her stool and resting her chin between her two palms, "I might think of something. Let me see now. What is there?"

There was silence for nearly a minute. Coleman's heavy breathing could be heard distinctly. Then the mother sat up suddenly, slapped her knees with her palms and cried: "Children, I have it. I have it. Get me my shawl quickly. Jump up, girls, and get me my shawl. Get me my shawl and my new check apron."

She jumped up, and taking a tiny portion of her black, threadbare skirt between the thumb and forefinger of each hand daintily, she jerked her head to one side and began to dance around the room, singing as she danced: "There was an old peddler in love with a nun, God forgive him."

They brought her shawl and the check apron and pestered her with questions, asking her what she was going to do, but she never budged.

"Now let me alone, children," she said, "let my blood be on my own hands. You just stay quiet in the house and if I am not back within two hours with food and the makings of a drink, ye will know where to find me, and that will be in the police barracks."

Then she put on her apron and her black shawl, which she wore in triangular fashion, with the point of it tipping the ground behind her heels, like a steering gear. She went out, marched through the village without looking at a person, with her shawl thrown far forward over her head, and stooping slightly. She walked down the road to the next village, which was a mile away, and where Mrs Murtagh had a little general shop, that sold everything which a peasant could be expected to buy, and bought everything which a peasant could be induced to sell, except cattle, of course, and immortal souls. It was a two-storied concrete house, and even though it was only three years old it looked bedraggled and weatherstained like a ship that had been away somewhere for a long time and has come back to port covered with barnacles and scratched and wicked-looking. Mrs Deignan marched into the hall and turned to her left, into the large, long dark room that served as the shop. There was a heavy smell of sugar, soap, salty bacon, and stale biscuits all mixed up together. Behind the counter, with her arms folded on her breast, stood Mrs Murtagh. She was a handsome woman of forty-five, with a pair of hard, mercenary eyes, with a foxy look in them. Her face would have been very beautiful were it not for that foxy look in her eyes and the yellowish colour of her skin around her cheeks. Her cheeks had a rosy flush like a young girl. She looked at Mrs Deignan furtively, and nodded her head slightly, as if she were not a bit pleased to see that good woman.

"Well," she said, in a very curt voice and with a very gross attempt at speaking in a humorous voice, "I suppose you have come to settle up that little bill you owe me. There, now, I always said your were an honest woman, Mrs Deignan. But sure don't be in a hurry with it. Let it lie another five years." She began to laugh in a queer manner that she had, a laugh that was almost like a hen's cackle, saving the comparison.

But the laugh died in her mouth when she saw the expression on Mrs Deignan's face. Mrs Murtagh was a hard woman, and could drive a hard bargain with a parish priest, such was her force of character, but still ... the look on Mrs Deignan's face terrified her. Mrs Deignan had not spoken a word. She had merely let her shawl fall back from her shoulder and trail behind her. She had let her lean, wrinkled, yellow-skinned hands go limp. She had allowed her face to go lax and loose and then gradually it began to curl and form convolutions like milk just getting ready to boil in a saucepan on a slow fire. Gradually her face gathered itself together, her throat became alive, her bosom gave signs that something devilish was forcing its way upwards from her middle and finding great difficulty in reaching her throat. In fact, Mrs Deignan looked as if she was going to give birth to something awful. She did. She began to talk. The first word came out with great difficulty, emerging from her wrinkled yellow lips in curves and spirals, with the grinding sound of a knife being sharpened on a whetstone. Then her words began to gather speed until they came pouring out of her mouth, with the sweet, sharp cadence of a rushing stream.

"Hypocrite, robber, receiver of stolen goods," she cried. "Oh, woman that has denied God, virtue, charity, and all the good deeds of the holy ones, you female devil routed from hell because Lucifer himself couldn't sleep under the same roof with such an abomination, you virago of the seven tongues, and they all cancerous with the load of foul words that come each hour across their flabby and pestilential backs; oh, daughter, shared by seven fathers and they all drunkards and vagabonds; oh, monster, oh! ... ah!" She paused, and raised her hands and held them in front of her face like an Eastern merchant going to strike a bargain. Her eyes distended, and she frothed at the mouth, "my tongue refuses to describe you." Suddenly she flopped down in a chair that stood by the counter and she began to fan herself with a corner of her shawl, while her whole body shook as if she were in hysterics.

"Is it out of your mind you are?" gasped Mrs Murtagh, in a low voice. She was beside herself with rage, but she was a cautious woman and fear gained the mastery of her rage. She stood behind the counter, trembling and darting her eyes out of the window for fear a customer might come in and hear Mrs Deignan. "Is it out of your mind you are?" she repeated. "What have you got against me? What is it I say? Speak, woman."

Mrs Deignan kept shaking her head and her right hand for a few moments, then she tried to open her lips, but she didn't. Encouraged by Mrs Deignan's failure to open her lips, Mrs Murtagh darted around the corner of the counter, folded her arms and glared at Mrs Deignan with ferocity.

"Speak," she hissed, "and say your say, or your bones will rot in jail while I have a pound to bribe a judge to keep you there."

"Ah-h-h-h-h-h." Mrs Deignan had opened her lips at last and given vent to a snarl like a dog. Her face became alive again and gathered in a ball. Her limp, little body became as active and mobile as a squirrel's body. Mrs Murtagh stepped back and, in spite of herself, she uttered a scream. "You would, would you?" cried Mrs Deignan. "You're a widow yourself, but you would stamp on another widow. We'll see-e-e-e, we'll se-e-e-e." Then she laughed loudly, ending her laugh in a high note that she changed in some manner into a scream of triumph. Then she bent forward her head and, with her hands on her knees, she looked into Mrs Murtagh's face and said, in a low distinct voice: "Where is the red petticoat you were wearing last Sunday night, when you went to visit the tailor?"

"Oh, Lord in heaven!" gasped Mrs Murtagh, putting her two clenched hands to her lips. Then she laughed in a hard, cold way that was quite artificial, and looked about her. Mrs Deignan kept glaring at her. Then she stopped laughing, gave a little start, and came up to Mrs Deignan and bent down to her and hissed straight at her: "You're a liar, I wasn't wearing a red petticoat last Sunday."

"You-are-telling-a-lie." Mrs Deignan shot out the words separately like a schoolmaster explaining something to a stupid boy. "I saw you with my own eyes coming out of the tailor's house wearing a red petticoat. Deny it if you can."

"It's a lie," cried Mrs Murtagh, suddenly straightening herself and stamping her foot. She was blood-red to the roots of her neck. "It's a lie," she cried again, in a short voice. "It wasn't a red petticoat I was wearing. It was a black skirt."

Mrs Deignan uttered an exclamation and jumped to her feet. Her face was radiant with delight.

"Ha," she cried, in a low, strident voice, just like the sound a man might make after swallowing a rich bottle of Guinness's stout on a very hot day. "Now, I have you. So it was you who was there, was it? I saw the black skirt as I was coming along the lane, but I wasn't sure. Ha-a-a-a-a. Didn't I find you out easily, my fine trapster? Didn't I?"

"Oh-h-h-h," hissed Mrs Murtagh through her teeth, as she rushed at Mrs Deignan. There was a tussle and a few screams and more curses, and the two women were at one another's throats, tearing at one another like a pair of cats that have met on a moonlight night in a back garden. Things were thrown about and there was considerable noise until at last Mrs Murtagh swung her enemy and sent her reeling to the far end of the shop, where she fell against a few sacks of flour. She was going to follow up her advantage when her habitual caution again gained control of her and she paused, looking undecidedly at Mrs Deignan. Mrs Deignan, who was not at all hurt, saw her indecision out of the corner of her eye. She promptly, in the very act of getting to her feet and assuming a posture of defence, threw her hands in the air and fell in a dead faint on the floor. As she fell, she muttered distinctly and audibly that she was "dead".

"Good God, what have I done?" cried Mrs Murtagh. "I've killed her." She rushed over to Mrs Deignan and raised her up. At the same moment two women appeared at the door of the shop attracted by the noise.

"God between us and all harm," cried one of them, "what is it?"

"It's a fit she has," whispered Mrs Murtagh. "Give me a hand to take her into the parlour, poor woman; it's her stomach is bad."

"Ah, God help the poor," said the two neighbours with insincerity, looking at one another with a look that said plainer than words that Mrs Murtagh had refused poor Mrs Deignan credit for some food and that Mrs Deignan had very properly assaulted her for such cruelty.

However, when they revived Mrs Deignan on the parlour sofa with smelling salts and a nip of brandy the two neighbours were bitterly disappointed to find the poor woman very grateful to Mrs Murtagh for her kindness. Mrs. Deignan sat up, rubbed her eyes with both hands, then her cheeks, then her chest, and then held out both hands to Mrs Murtagh. With tears visible in her eyes, she looked at Mrs Murtagh and said: "Oh, may God in heaven reward you for your kindness to the poor. Neighbours", she cried, turning to the two other women, "it's how I came in here and told her that we didn't have a bite of food in the house for the past week, not even a bite of a potato to give to the four poor orphans that the Lord gave to me as a burden. And, like the good woman that she is, she turned around and said, said she: 'Mrs Deignan, put your shawl on the counter and I'll give for the honour of God, what'll stop the cry of hunger in your house for a few days, tea and sugar and flour, and whatever you like to take on six months' credit.' Ah-h-h-h-h, neighbours, it was too much for me. It was too much for me. Ba-a-a-a-h, it was too much for me. I took bad. Ba-a-a-a-h." And she began to beat her middle with both hands.

The two women went out and whispered to one another outside that there was something in the wind. But what it was they couldn't make out. And they went home in a vile temper.

Ten minutes later, Mrs Deignan emerged with her black shawl turned into a wallet laid across her back, and in the round, black bottom of the shawl there were two pounds of sugar, a pound of tea, four tins of condensed milk, two stone of flour, and four loaves that had gone a bit stale. And at the door of the shop stood Mrs Murtagh looking after her customer with a look of bitter hatred. But her fear was stronger than her hatred. The one black spot on her character, her illicit affair with the bachelor tailor, was discovered by this virago of a poetess. And Mrs Murtagh kept thinking of the number of times Mrs Deignan would go away with a shawl full of groceries on her. But then, again, she thought of the tailor.

Biographical Notes

Liam O'Flaherty was born in 1897 into an Irish-speaking community on the Aran Islands, off the west coast of Ireland. He was the ninth of ten children, who all had to be supported on 15 acres of rocky land. When he was 13, he was recruited by visiting priests to be trained for the priesthood in their college on the mainland; but at 17, he decided against becoming a priest and studied classics at University College, Dublin on a scholarship instead.

On the outbreak of the first World War, he broke off his studies and volunteered to fight with the Irish Guards. After two years of trench warfare on the continent, he returned, wounded and badly shell-shocked, to the Aran Islands, where he began to write. It was not long, however, until he became restless again, and set out to travel widely in Europe and America, working at all sorts of odd jobs. About this time he became a communist, though he later abandoned this ideology. In 1922 he was back in Ireland, and fought in the Civil War on the radical Republican side. He wrote some stories about this period, but soon reverted to writing about the kind of life he knew best – that of the Aran Islands. A number of these were written in Irish.

He achieved considerable commercial success in the decades which followed. His novel The Informer *was made into a Hollywood film. He lived in the United States for a number of years and travelled widely. In spite of all this, he never lost contact with the simple life he had known as a boy. What Dublin was for James Joyce, Aran was, and still is, for Liam O'Flaherty. In his best stories, whether they deal with people, or (as is often the case) animals, he concentrates on depicting simple, basic emotions: parental love, fear, the struggle for survival. The story we have chosen is quite typical of his work in this respect. It also admits a glimpse of a way of life which, though it now belongs to the past, has strongly influenced the development of modern Ireland, and in particular, its popular culture and literature.*

Annotations

26 **Liam** ['lɪəm] *Gael.* form of 'William' – **O'Flaherty** [əʊ'flæhətɪ / oː'flæhərtɪ] – **petticoat** *here:* full skirt (Red petticoats with black shawls were traditional dress of women in the west of Ireland.) – 1 **Deignan** ['daɪgnən] – 2 **cabin** *here:* very simple cottage – 4 **oaten cake** bread made from oats (Hafer) – 5 **to give out** to be used up – 6 **Coleman** anglicized version of *Gael.* 'Colmán' – 7 **pickle** liquid containing salt, vinegar etc. for preserving foods – 11 **to forage** ['fɒrɪdʒ] to search (for food, etc.) – 20 **frieze** [friːz] thick woollen cloth – 23 **stock** animals kept for meat, milk, etc. – 24 **odd job** occasional work – 25 **to scrub** [ʌ] to clean thoroughly – 28 **indigent** ['– – –] poor – 29 **for a spell** for a certain length of time

27 1 **Divine** godly – **capacity** ability – 4 **settle** long wooden seat with high back and arms – 6 **flatulence** gas in the stomach – 7 **like a possessed one** as if possessed by the devil – 9 **at the end of their tether** ['teðə(r)] at their wit's end, not knowing what to do next – **their credit was exhausted** they could no longer buy without paying immediately – 10 **sty** house where pigs are kept – **in lieu of** instead of, in place of – **Flanagan** ['– – –] – **Kilmurrage** [–'– –] – 11 **Co. Mayo** county in the north-west – 16 **turf** *Ir.* peat, used in Ireland for burning in open fires – 18 **to weave (wove, woven)** to twist together – **plait**

[æ] three or more lengths of hair woven together like a rope – 20 **stubby** short and thick – 23 **blaze** fire, flames – 26 **slender** thin – 33 **form** long wooden bench – **to brood** to think deeply

28 6 **Inverara** [ˌ– –ˈ– –] – 7 **scurrilous** [ʌ] rude and insulting – **abusive** insulting – 8 **indecent** obscene – 10 **to droop** to hang loosely – 24 **check** with a pattern of squares – 25 **threadbare** worn thin – 26 **daintily** in an elegant, 'refined' way – 28 **peddler** person who sells from house to house – 29 **to pester** to annoy by repeating questions, etc. – 30 **not to budge** to remain firm – 34 **barracks** [ˈbærɪks] *Ir.* police station – 37 **steering gear** rudder, underwater part of ship which controls direction – 39 **to stoop** to bend down – 40 **Murtagh** [ˈmɜː(r)tə]

29 1 **peasant** [ˈpezənt] poor country man or woman – 3 **immortal** living for ever – 4 **bedraggled** untidy – 6 **barnacles** shell-fish that cling to ships – 11 **mercenary** [ˈ– – – –] interested mainly in making money – 12 **foxy** clever, calculating – 14 **furtive** secretive, as if hiding s.th. – 17 **curt** hard, unfriendly – **gross** [əʊ] vulgar, coarse – 22 **cackle** sound made by a hen – **saving ...** if you will excuse me for ... – 24 **could drive a hard bargain with a parish priest** hard enough to do business with anyone (P.P. as a respected figure of authority) – 28 **lean** thin – **limp, lax** weak, loose – 30 **convolutions** twists and turns – 37 **whetstone** stone for sharpening knives – 39 **cadence** [ˈkeɪdəns] flowing, rhythmic sound – 40 **hypocrite** [ˈhɪpəkrɪt] insincere person

30 1 **to deny God** to betray, to reject God – 2 **to rout** [aʊ] to force out of a place – 3 **abomination** horrible person, monster – **virago** [vɪˈrɑːgəʊ] violent, bad-tempered woman – 5 **flabby** loose – **pestilential** diseased – 8 **to distend** to open wide – 9 **to froth** to produce foam (small bubbles) – 10 **to flop** to fall loosely – **to fan o.s.** to produce a light wind to cool o.s. – 11 **in hysterics** hysterical, with no control over one's behaviour – 13 **Is it ... you are?** *Ir. coll.* (transl. from Gaelic) Are you ...? – 14 **beside herself** on the point of losing her self-control – **cautious** very careful – 15 **to dart** to make quick movements – 22 **to glare** to stare angrily – 23 **ferocity** violent anger – 24 **to rot** to go bad – 25 **to bribe** to give money in order to influence s.o. illegally – 26 **to give vent to** to let out – 27 **snarl** sound expressing great anger

31 13 **strident** harsh, hard – 14 **Guinness** [ˈgɪnəs] brand name – **stout** a very dark beer – 17 **trapster** [ˈtreɪpstə(r)] person who moves around casually – 19 **tussle** [ʌ] fight – 23 **to reel** to stagger, to move in circles because of dizziness – 28 **posture** position, way of standing – 29 **to fall in a faint** to become unconscious – **to mutter** to speak in a very low voice – 30 **audible** can be heard – 35 **fit** a sudden attack of an illness – 40 **to assault** to attack

32 1 **parlour** 'best room' of a house or cottage – **smelling salts** substance used to revive s.o. – 20 **in a vile temper** very angry or upset – 22 **wallet** *here:* bag – 24 **stone** unit of weight (14 pounds) – 27 **illicit** not in accordance with moral or social laws – **bachelor** unmarried man

Interpretation and Teaching Notes

Background, Content and Analysis

The role of the Gaelic story-telling tradition in the emergence of the modern Irish short story is still a matter of debate. One of the more plausible – and empirically verifiable – evaluations of the influence of such a tradition is that the short story tends to flourish "in those countries where a vibrant oral culture is suddenly challenged by the onset of a sophisticated literary tradition"[1]. If this is true, then Liam O'Flaherty was well placed to make a unique contribution to its development.

"A Red Petticoat" gives a fair representation of the kind of community the author grew up in[2]: impoverished and in many ways primitive, but enlivened by just such a "vibrant oral culture". The Deignan family of the story were by no means unique in their artistic endeavours. In the days before the advent of radio, the gramophone, and later television, the everyday entertainment of peasant communities in the West of Ireland consisted of conversation, poetry-reciting, storytelling, traditional music and dancing.

Apparently the O'Flaherty home was one of those houses where people liked to gather round the fire especially on winter evenings. Liam O'Flaherty's father was an excellent dancer, and his mother was noted for her singing and storytelling. Liam O'Flaherty's own description of his mother indicates that she was his model for at least the more admirable side of Mary Deignan's character:

> Her life was a tale of hardship and misery, an endless struggle to find food for her many children. And yet how gay she was in spite of all her suffering! Even when there was no food in the house, she would gather us about her at the empty hearth and weave fantastic stories about giants and fairies, or mime the comic adventures of our neighbours, until our hungry little bellies were sick with laughter. No suffering could dull the divine enthusiasm with which life inspired her.[3]

When confronted in the course of his studies and travels with a "sophisticated literary tradition", Liam O'Flaherty experimented briefly with a var-

1 Declan Kiberd, "Story-Telling: The Gaelic Tradition" in *The Irish Short Story*, ed. Rafroidi

2 Cf. J. M. Synge, *The Aran Islands*

3 Liam O'Flaherty, *Shame the Devil*

iety of themes and forms, but soon discovered the subject-matter appropriate to his own vision of humanity among the people of Aran. Not only that, but he also adopted many of the formal elements of the oral story-telling tradition in his writing.

The 'oral' nature of the narrative of "A Red Petticoat" is evident from the start. The 'incomplete' sentences of the first paragraph (ll. 2–3, 8–9) give the impression of being 'afterthoughts' in an improvised fireside tale. The rather unusual phrasing of the first of these examples is also an indication that both narrative and dialogue are intended to approximate the phrasing, syntax and idioms of the Irish spoken on Aran. (Some further examples of Gaelic-influenced syntax: p. 26, ll. 18–19; p. 27, ll. 1–2; p. 28, l. 40; p. 30, l. 13; p. 31, ll. 35, 36; p. 32, l. 8.)

The digressions of the third paragraph, and especially the reference to "the father, old Mick Deignan" (which becomes so extended that the introductory "since" has to be repeated, ll. 18, 21), are also typical of Gaelic story-telling, at least in the more popular form practised by the type of story-teller known as the *seanchaí* [ˌʃanəˈxiː].

Unlike the *scéalaí* [ˌʃkeəˈliː], who enjoyed a somewhat higher status and specialized in elaborate traditional tales of fixed form, the *seanchaí* was expected to spin his or her narratives out of the material of everyday life, linking them with the names of real people and familiar places, and giving the impression of having witnessed the events personally – or at least of having reliable sources. Such is the cumulative effect of the mass of detail given at the beginning of the story.

Identifying the narrator as a story-teller in the Gaelic tradition necessarily implies a corresponding audience. The reader may indeed get the impression of listening in on a fireside gathering of people who share the cultural attitudes and assumptions of the story-teller, as well as a certain store of knowledge – e.g. of the economics of village life (e.g. p. 26, l. 26), or of the features and habits of old Mick Deignan (ll. 18–21). Though most readers are unlikely to share this common background, the narrator's assumption that they do lends an illusion of reality to the actual telling of the story which makes the factual or fictional nature of the tale itself irrelevant. We are encouraged to put ourselves in the position of the *seanchaí*'s audience and enjoy the story for its own sake.

The Deignan family is presented in the story as an extreme example of the traditional way of life on Aran: living from hand to mouth, working when absolutely necessary, but otherwise trusting to providence (p. 26, l. 10 – p. 27, l. 7). The extreme nature of their happy-go-lucky attitude allows the narrator to criticize them for being "lazy and indigent" (p. 26, l. 28).

One notices, however, a certain sympathy and even admiration for this "remarkable" family (ll. 17–18) with their "divine capacity for enjoying life" (p. 27, l. 1), the suggestion being that the "rage" felt by the villagers (p. 26, l. 32) is based on envy.

The same ambivalence applies to the characterization of Mary Deignan as an individual. In calling her "Mary of the Bad Verses", the villagers may be expressing disapproval of the immorality of her verses, but such epithets are normally awarded to the more interesting characters in the community.

After an extended exposition in which the family background and their present economic dilemma ("no food in the house", p. 26, l. 3) is presented, the narrator finally gets around to dealing with the obvious question: what are they going to do? One gets the impression here that many of the digressions (especially p. 27, ll. 17–38) were deliberate delaying tactics on the part of the narrator for the purpose of building up tension. When it emerges that the mother does have a plan to save her family from starvation, we are not told what it is, only that it is one which might get her put in prison (p. 28, ll. 31–34). As it turns out, the song she sings at this point (ll. 27–28) contains a suggestion of her actual plan. Even if this hint is not immediately understood, it adds to the listener's or reader's impression that something of questionable morality is planned.

Then comes a detailed description of Mary Deignan's walk to the next village and Mrs Murtagh's general shop, where the remainder of the action takes place. It soon becomes obvious that whatever plan Mary Deignan has thought up to save her family from starvation, it will be at the expense of Mrs Murtagh. The shopkeeper is described in predominantly negative terms (p. 29, ll. 9–22): "a handsome woman" but with "hard mercenary eyes", "foxy", "a queer manner", a laugh "like a hen's cackle", etc. This may be rather unfair to Mrs Murtagh, but the story-teller can probably count on the complicity of his or her implied listeners: in a rural community in the west of Ireland, it was not uncommon for the village shopkeeper to be an unpopular character, seen as exploiting the economically weak for his or her own profit.

Mrs Murtagh's sarcastic reference to Mrs Deignan's debts is met by a performance which even exceeds what we have already been told about her extraordinary talents. First it is her facial expression which terrifies the shopkeeper. This is described in a series of colourful imagery (ll. 26–39) which testifies to the high level of expressive ability in Irish-speaking communities. Mary Deignan finally does "give birth to something awful" – a string of fanciful insults of such an appalling nature that it is only caution which prevents Mrs Murtagh from retaliating in kind.

Then Mrs Deignan gets to the point: by pretending to inquire about the red petticoat she claims to have seen Mrs Murtagh wearing when coming from the tailor's house on Sunday, she tricks her into admitting she was there, but wearing a black skirt. Now Mrs Murtagh realizes that Mary Deignan knows about her illicit affair with the tailor. At this, Mrs Murtagh loses her self-control and a tussle ensues which ends with Mary Deignan pretending to faint. She comes to in the presence of two neighbours who had been attracted by the noise. Assuming that the poor woman has been cruelly refused credit by the shopkeeper, they are astonished to find Mrs Deignan apparently grateful to Mrs Murtagh, whose generosity, she exclaims, was too much for her (p. 32, ll. 6–17). Only one course of action is now open to the shopkeeper: she must go along with this interpretation, and supply the Deignan family with the food they so badly need. Mary Deignan's trick has succeeded.

Throughout this farcical scene, the humour is clearly on the side of Mrs Deignan, in spite of the questionable morality of her behaviour. One gets the impression that the narrator (or even the author) is not thinking in terms of 'right' and 'wrong' any more than Mary Deignan herself. We are given no direct access to her thoughts and feelings (the possible implication being that in a situation of such elementary need, an analysis of psychological states can tell us no more than the situation itself implies), but her behaviour seems to indicate that she has no conventional sense of morality and no sense of guilt. Her 'morality' – such as it is – could be summed up as follows: 'right' is what increases the well-being of herself and her family, or (in bad times) ensures their survival; 'wrong' is unhappiness, failure, hunger. In this she could be compared to certain other O'Flaherty protagonists: those of "The Wild Goat's Kid" or "The Hawk", for example. Like his animal stories, "A Red Petticoat" testifies to the author's fascination with, and admiration for "the free, the flawless, the ecstatically abandoned, the amoral exultant spirit ... perfect embodiments of energy"[4].

4 Brendan Kennelly, "Liam O'Flaherty: A View of His Short Stories" in *The Irish Short Story*, ed. Rafroidi

First Unit
The Setting of the Story

Preparation: The students should have read at least to page 28, line 34.

1. First three pages as 'exposition'.
Say where the 'action' of the story starts – and describe the contents of the story up to that point.
Page 28, either line 29 or 35; up to that point, introduction to the Deignan family, their way of life, their economic situation, the kind of society they live in and their position in the community, i.e. an extended exposition.

2. How the setting is established
What details in the opening paragraph indicate the particular setting of the story? Can you identify the geographical location?
"... sitting around the fire ... cabin ... oaten cake ... dried fish ..."
These details indicate a setting which is unfamiliar to most readers; living conditions seem to be primitive. Identifiable to the informed ("Introductory Lesson" should suffice!) as one of the remoter coastal areas of the West of Ireland.

3. Comparison with setting of O'Connor story
How does the setting differ – geographically, historically and socially – from the setting of "Guests of the Nation"?

	"Guests"	"Red Petticoat"
geographically:	vague, anywhere in rural Ireland	remote west coast or islands
historically:	fight for independence 1918–21	vague, probably early 20th c. (could be same period)
socially:	abnormal war situation	normal, everyday life

(Note: In the O'Connor story, the 'old woman' provides a link with the world of O'Flaherty's characters.)

4. The Deignans' way of life
What do we learn about the Deignan family and their relationship with the other villagers?
The Deignans are described as living from hand to mouth, working at odd jobs when absolutely necessary, but otherwise trusting to providence (p. 26 l. 10 – p. 27, l. 7). In spite of their extreme poverty they are happy and enjoy life, spending a lot of their time "composing poems, cracking jokes" etc. (p. 26, ll. 30–31, p. 27, ll. 12–14, 28–29). The villagers envy them for this,

and at least some of them are hostile (p. 26, l. 31 – p. 27, l. 4, ll. 9–11); the mother's epithet 'Mary of the Bad Verses', however, also suggests a certain admiration for her as an interesting personality.

Homework: Read to end.

Second Unit
The Central Character and her Morality

1. Summary of the action

What has the song Mary Deignan sings on p. 28, ll. 27–28, got to do with her plan to save her family from starvation? How successful is this plan?

The song about an illicit love affair suggests her actual plan: to blackmail a local shopkeeper into supplying them with food. The plan is successful: by pretending to have seen Mrs Murtagh visiting the tailor wearing a red petticoat, she tricks her into admitting that she was there, wearing a black skirt; in the row which ensues, Mrs Deignan pretends to faint; when she comes to, in the presence of two neighbours, she pretends it was out of astonishment at Mrs Murtagh's generosity in extending her unlimited credit.

2. Characterization of Mary Deignan – direct and indirect

What does Mary Deignan's successful scheme reveal of her character? How does this fit in with what the narrator tells us?

Her plan reveals that she is cunning, ingenious and completely unscrupulous. Her execution of the plan shows that she is also a good actress, fluent, articulate, with a very sharp tongue (indirect characterization). Her verbal proficiency and her skilful use of it as a weapon were mentioned earlier by the narrator (p. 28, ll. 5–8); also – "remarkable", "lazy" (p. 26, ll. 17, 27) (direct characterization).

3. Mary Deignan's morality – the principle of survial

We learn a lot about Mary Deignan's social and linguistic skills, and about her actual behaviour. But what about her feelings, her motivation, her sense of morality?

Nothing is told of her feelings beyond brief references to the family's 'misery' (p. 26, l. 2). The predicament of her family implies motivation enough – there is no need for subtle analysis of psychological states.

Her behaviour seems to indicate that she has no conventional sense of morality: 'right' is what saves herself and her family from starvation, 'wrong' is failure, hunger. She also lacks a sense of guilt – no feeling that she is partly to blame for the family's situation. Her main aims: (in good times) well-being, pleasure; (in bad times) survival.

4. The author's attitude to Mary Deignan's behaviour
Do you think the author approves or disapproves of such behaviour? How can you discern his attitude?
Indications of approval:
- the fact that the author lets her succeed in her plan at the expense of someone who is herself not morally blameless
- humour is on the side of Mrs Deignan (esp. p. 31, l. 31 – end)

Indication of disapproval:
- direct reference to Mrs Deignan's negative characteristics (e.g. "lazy", p. 26, l. 28; "immoral" verses, p. 28, l. 8)

Conclusion: either approval, on balance – or neutrality, as if conventional morality is not applicable here.

Homework: Re-read the story, and decide who the narrator might be. (Consider the narrative technique and the language used in the story.)

Third Unit
The Narrator

1. Evidence of spoken language in the narrative
What is unusual about the language of the narrative? Concentrate on the first page.
Several grammatically 'incomplete' sentences, either reduced to a single subordinate clause or to a mere phrase (ll. 8–9); repetitions (ll. 17–18); frequent use of "and" to link sentences and clauses (e.g. ll. 18, 21); the expression "to tell the truth" (l. 27) – all evidence of spoken, not written language.
(Some of these structures sound particularly strange because they are the author's attempt to represent spoken Irish – the language of the community described here – in English, e.g. "For the reason that . . .", ll. 2–3.)

2. Narrative technique
Considering that the narrative consists of spoken language, which of the following possibilities comes closest to the situation in the story –
a) the author speaking directly to the reader?
b) somebody relating what he or she has personally observed?
c) somebody relating what he or she has learnt from various sources?

The 'spoken' nature of the language makes a) unlikely; b) impossible – nobody could have observed all of the action; c) comes closest, though the details given of dialogue and private thoughts of the characters go far beyond what could be learned from any sources – this "somebody" assumes a certain degree of omniscience, i.e. uses imagination.

3. The narrator as 'story-teller' in the Gaelic tradition
Re-examine the passage on page 26, ll. 16–27 for an indication of the narrator's relationship with the community described, and for an indication of who he or she is telling the story to.
A great number of details are mentioned which suggest total familiarity with the way of life described, such as one would expect from one of the villagers themselves. The seemingly irrelevant details about "old Mick Deignan" seem to be addressed to some listeners who may have known the old man. All in all, one gets the impression that this is a tale told by one of the villagers to some others.
Is there a hint in the story itself that such 'story-telling' is likely?
Mary Deignan's "bad verses" and her family's custom of "composing poems, cracking jokes" etc. suggest a lively oral culture in the community described.

For Further Study

Courses/Projects based on this story

1. Stories by Liam O'Flaherty
"A Red Petticoat" plus a selection from the Longman Imprint paperback *The Wave and Other Stories,* or at least three of the following, all from *The Short Stories of Liam O'Flaherty* (Jonathan Cape):
- "The Wild Goat's Kid"
- "His First Flight" – also included in *Twelve Short Masterpieces* (Klett)
- "The Fairy Goose"
- "The Sniper" – also included in *Contemporary British Short Stories* (Hueber) and *Loves, Hopes and Fears* (Longman Imprint); simplified version included in *Learning English, Compact Course 4* (Klett)
- "Civil War" – also included in *Ireland: History and Present State* (Diesterweg)
- "Going Into Exile" – also included in *Irish Short Stories* (Schöningh); extracts included in *Ireland: History and Present State* (Diesterweg) and Topical Texts 16: *Ireland and Its Problems* (Klett)

- "Red Barbara" – also available on record, read by the author (Claddagh Records, CCT 15–16)

2. The Aran Islands
- "A Red Petticoat"
- Extracts from J. M. Synge, *The Aran Islands* (Oxford Paperback)
- A play by J. M. Synge, either *Riders to the Sea* (a one-acter) or *The Playboy of the Western World* (Penguin: *Classic Irish Drama*)
- If possible, see and discuss the film *Man of Aran* (1934) directed by Robert Flaherty – no relation.
- Collect information on the Aran Islands today from reference books.

3. Irish Folk Traditions
- "A Red Petticoat"
- A selection from *The Children of the Salmon and Other Irish Folktales,* ed. Eileen O'Faolain, or from *Folktales of the Irish Countryside,* ed. Kevin Danaher, Mercier pb. 1967
- Listen to some records of traditional Irish music. A large selection is available; the following are mentioned because they are both traditional in style, and include songs sung in the English language: The Chieftans, *Bonaparte's Retreat* (Claddagh Records CC 20); Dolores Keane, *There Was a Maid* (Claddagh CC 23). Though mixed in style, any recordings by the groups 'Clannad', 'Planxty', 'The Bothy Band' will give an impression of Irish music today; similarly the urbanized 'Folk' of such groups as 'The Dubliners'.

Sean O'Faolain

The Man Who Invented Sin

In our youth when we used to pour into the mountains to learn Irish, places that were lonely and silent for the rest of the year became full of gaiety during the summer months. Every day there were picnics and expeditions; every night there were dances, moonlight boating parties, singsongs in the cottages. The village street became a crowded promenade; its windows never went black before one in the morning; the pub was never empty. Where once you could have been utterly alone half a mile off the road, in the bog or up the mountain, you could not now be sure of privacy anywhere. If you went up the mountain to bathe naked in some tiny loch you might suddenly see a file of young students like Alpineers coming laughing down on you over the next scarp; you might turn the corner of a lonely mountain pass courting your girl and burst upon a bevy of nuns sedately singing choruses among the rocks – for every kind of teacher, laymen and women, nuns, priests, and monks were encouraged in those years to come out into the hills.

How we all got accommodation I do not know. The priests took lodgings in the villages. The monks and nuns purchased derelict houses which had been abandoned by the landlords after the Revolution. The people gave up their best rooms to the rest of us, turned lofts into dormitories, one or two even set up secondhand bell tents. One July, so stifling was the house where I stayed – six at least to every room – that I used to take a rug every night and climb into the high hay in the barn; and there were always four or five like me who preferred to be bitten by the ticks and waked early by the birds and the mountain air than to be half suffocated in featherbeds under the baking slates. By the end of the month, however, I got so tired of digging the little crablike ticks from under my skin that I moved two miles out the road to a place called Ryder's, a small house on the lower lake, which usually took nobody at all. Indeed, only by great cajoling did I persuade Mrs Ryder to take me in. My only fear, then, was that I might be lonely. But before she knew what had happened Mr Ryder had not merely one lodger but five; for with the beginning of August the monks' hostel overflowed, and the nuns' hostel overflowed, and she had to take in two of the monks and two of the nuns.

There was nothing remarkable about my fellow students, except, perhaps, that little Sister Magdalen was so dainty and gay and spirited that it seemed a shame to lock her away from the world in a convent. Sister Chrysostom was tall, delicate, with big hands and a blotchy skin, and she walked with her toes turned in. She was a bit of a Miss Prim, and I think she had been chosen as companion for Sister Magdalen because she was so prim. Brother Virgilius was a countryman with a powerful frame and a powerful voice, round red cheeks, and no nerves, and why he had chosen to be a monk was hard to understand. It seemed to me that he would have made a better farmer than a teacher. However, I found that he was a fine hurler and I am sure the boys loved him for his natural ways. Brother Majellan was very different, a gentle, apple-cheeked man with big glasses, a complexion like a girl's, teeth as white as a hound's, and soft, beaming eyes. He was an intelligent, sensitive man. I took to him immediately.

At first we saw very little of one another. They had their principal meal at their own hostels, were studying most of the day, and the only time we all met was in the evenings, when we sat in the little garden and passed discreet remarks across the path about politics or the weather; or, if there was rain, we would meet in the drawing room, where there was a turf fire, and talk of the day's lessons. They kept convent hours, were off to their rooms by nine at the latest, and long before I rose were gone down to the village to morning Mass. That year, however, the weather broke suddenly in the middle of August so that we found ourselves in the drawing room almost every evening, over our notebooks and dictionaries and grammars. We had, by then, become like travellers on a long railway journey who have broken the silence and are beginning to chat companionably. We might still sit silent for, say, a quarter of an hour, but then somebody would say something and we would all get going. One night, for instance, Majellan lifted his eager, earnest, doggy eyes, and said: "Sister Magdalen, how do you pronounce the word which I call *cearrbhach*?"

"Oh, Brother Majellan," she laughed, shocked at herself, entertained by her own folly, "I am afraid I do not even know what the word means!"

Virgilius clapped his two big countryman's paws together and roared out laughing.

"Sister Magdalen, I'm surprised at you! I'm surprised at you! Not know the word *cearrbhach?* It means a card player or a gambler."

"And is that what it means? *Cearrbhach.*" And she pronounced the guttural word as daintily as if it rhymed with *peruke.*

She was a city girl and had never before heard Irish spoken by anybody but city people.

"No! Your're not saying it right at all. You're too ladylike about it. Say it the way the people say it. *This* way."

"I see." And again the dainty pronunciation like *peruke.* "Like that?"

"Listen, Sister. I'll show you the way to talk Irish. If you'll pardon the expression, make a great big shpit inside in your mouth and gurgle it. Like this: *carrwoochhhk.*"

Chrysostom immediately protested.

"Please, Brother Virgilius! If we cannot speak our own language like ladies let us not speak it at all."

"But," from Majellan, "that really is the way the people speak. It is a guttural language. Like German."

"Not Bavarian German. It is true that the Prussians . . ."

And off they went into a heated argument – the sort of argument we were always having in those days, about whether Ireland must always be a peasant country, and what other countries had achieved, and Virgilius, who hated arguments, blew out his lips and looked gloomily at his two big feet streched out before him, and Majellan and Magdalen got so excited that Chrysostom had to stop it with her usual:

"Sister, I really think it is our hour to retire."

*

One day at the college, as we called the sun-baked tin building where we studied from ten to one, we were asked to write an essay on a proverb to which the nearest Saxon equivalent is "The child is father to the man." I remember, that evening, how the mists lifted from the hills, and the sun began to raise gentle wisps of steam from the rocks, and the trout were leaping from a lake as blue as the patches of sky between the dissolving clouds. We spread newspapers on the two damp garden seats, and as we discussed the proper Irish terms to be used, the four of them began, without noticing it, to speak of their own childhood; where they had been born, where they went to school, and so on. Sister Magdalen sucked the end of her silver pencil and said:

"I know the Gaelic for 'I was born.' That is *Do rugadh mé.* And the place – Templemore. Of course, that is *An Teampall Mór.* The Great Temple. Or The Big Church. Though the Lord knows there's no big temple in Templemore." She sighed. Then she cocked her head suddenly. "I suppose you were never in Templemore, Brother Majellan? But, sure, why would you! It's an out-of-the-way litte place."

Chrysostom tapped my fingers irritably with her pencil. I was idly pulling a fuchsia flower to pieces.

"How would you say that, Sister?"

"Which? What? What was it you said, Sister Chrysostom?"

"'It's an out-of-the-way little place.' You see, I want to say that, too. I was born in a small little place like Templemore."

"Where was that?" asked Virgilius idly. He had been staring solemnly at the fuchsia that I threw into his lap.

"Kilfinane," said Chrysostom, "in County Limerick."

At once Virgilius whirled and slapped her thigh.

"Yerrah, Chrysostom, do you mean to tell me that you come from Kilfinane!"

"Brother!" And she held his arm excitedly. "Do you know Kilfinane?"

"Do I know my own father? Wasn't I born just below in Kilmallock? Oh, wisha, then, 'tis many the fine Sunday I took the old bicycle out to Kilfinane hunting hares behind the rath. If you come from Kilfinane you must surely know the rath?"

"The rath is on our land!"

"Ah, no?" – in a huge childish delight.

"Often and often I stood on the rath and looked down at the smoke of the train coming into Kilmallock – in and out of the woods – the little white smoke. And I could watch it again for another half an hour after it left Kilmallock, puffing away down towards Cork."

"I well believe you! It's a wonderful view. They say you can see six counties!"

"For a whole hour," she remembered. "The little white smoke. I used to wonder who might be in it, and would I ever travel away in it myself."

"Didn't I go every night to meet it at the station and gather the Dublin papers, for my uncle kept a paper shop in the Main Street? The Cork train we called it. Majellan, you're a Corkman, aren't you?"

Majellan was not listening to us. He was gazing across the darkening lake whose headlands were faint as smoke.

"My father," said Sister Magdalen thoughtfully, "was a doctor. I know how to say that, too. My mother died when I was fourteen. ... I was a lone child. ... My father married a second time."

Majellan kept staring over the lake. She said something about a notebook and flitted indoors. I got tired of listening to Virgilius and Chrysostom and got up to go to the dance. It was only then I noticed that Majellan and Magdalen were in the hall. She was dabbing her eyes with his big red handkerchief.

When I came back from the dance the half-moon had vaporized the moist land with a melancholy, filmy light. The house was black and silent.

*

I think it was Virgilius who first began to play pitch-and-toss along the garden path, and it was that evening that Magdalen called Majellan "Jelly". I came on them laughing over the game, which Brother Virgilius was trying to teach to the other three. Brother Majellan was, by then, calling Sister Magdalen "Maggie", Chrysostom naturally became "Chrissy", and Virgilius, of course, joined Jelly als "Jilly". How they laughed over that! I crowned the night for them by taking them up to the drawing-room piano and teaching them all a song with a chorus: *Bab Eró 'gus O mo mhíle grá.*

And Chrissy so surprised us by the strength and sweetness of her voice that at the end Virgilius clapped his hands and shouted, "I wouldn't doubt you, Chrissy. I knew you had it in you," and made her sing the song again alone. As she sang we heard a clear echo: it was a boating party out on the lake. They took up the chorus and gave it back to her until they faded around a headland still singing.

"But you know," gurgled Magdalen, "I really don't know what it all means. Can you translate it for me, Jelly?"

"No trouble at all," said Majellan. "It is a young fellow singing a song to his lady and this is what he says."

As he translated he gradually blushed redder and redder, and Virgilius winked at the big, rolling eyes of Magdalen, and her rounded little mouth, just ready to burst into laughter. When Majellan stuck his head right out through the window to look at the lake Magdalen burst. Chrysostom said, "I really think, Sister, it is our hour to retire."

"Jelly," said Virgilius, when they were gone, "you big gom! You have as much sense as a child of two."

When monks and nuns quarrel, I found, they seem to be astonished and shocked rather than angry: like children who have bumped against a door or a calf who has tried his first nettle. Grown men would have ended it with a curse or a clout. I escaped down to the kitchen to practise my Irish on Mrs Ryder. She was baking a cake, and humming *Bab Eró* ... Her cousin, who was the clerk in the post office, was sitting on the settle. She asked me which had the lovely voice. Mrs Ryder said her house was blessed.

"The creatures! Isn't it grand to hear them enjoying themselves? Four saints I have in the house."

"Only four?" I protested.

"What time did *you* come in last night?" she asked, and the conversation became exuberantly coarse.

The next evening, too, was exquisitely silent. The tiny trout splashes could be heard clearly, and the cattle lying on the dry strand across the water chewing the cud. We were all upstairs, I playing the piano, Virgilius seated in the open window singing and beating time with a silver tankard that young Ryder won in a tug of war, Jelly and Maggie trying to waltz, and when Chrissy was not laughing at poor Jelly's efforts to learn the steps she, too, was singing, at *Bab Eró,* like a blackbird. The music must have carried a long way over the water.

The door was slashed open with a bang that made the piano hum, and there was our local curate's black barrel of a body blocking the opening: for though he was not more than twenty-five – I believe it was his first parish – he was very fat. He was also pompous and cocksure. In the college we called him Lịspeen, which is the Irish for a frog. For that second it was as if a cinema reel stopped dead – the tankard held in the air, the two dancers like a waxworks, and Chrissy with her mouth open.

"Glory be to God," he moaned. "So I have been informed correctly." (It was only after that I thought of the postmistress on the settle the night before; you might as well talk to a microphone as to a postmistress.) "To think that this kind of thing has been going on under my nose for weeks." He let his voice fall solemnly, even secretively. "Unknown to anybody!" He roared then. "To think I cannot go for a summer walk to read my office without hearing this kind of caterwauling!" His voice fell again. "If Martin Luther could only see this! What's your name?" he stabbed at Chrissy. She had turned as pale as her coif.

"Sisster Chryssossostom, Father."

"And your name, Sister?"

"My name is Sister Mary Magdalen," said Maggie, very dignified and entirely self-possessed, and looking very angry.

"Well named," he growled. I saw Jelly grow red with fury. "Go to your rooms, please. I'll talk to these gentlemen." With a scornful emphasis on the last word.

They fluttered out obediently, Magdalen with her head in the air, Chrysostom with terror in her eyes. Majellan turned on him. I held his arm. He was only a monk, and no match for a curate in his own parish.

"You had no right, Father, to talk to the sisters like that."

The curate swelled.

"Are you daring to answer me back, young man?"

Majellan's voice shook, but he held his ground.

"We were doing no harm."

Even Virgilius spoke up, though more respectfully – he knew the power before him.

"Sure we were only having a bit of singsong, Father?"

The curate gasped, melodramatically – I swear he had taken a prize for elocution at his seminary – then dropped into a wonderful tone of sarcasm.

"Only having a bit of a singsong? *Only* having a bit of a singsong? Well, well!" He put his stick behind him like a shooting stick and teetered back and fro on it. He was very sure of himself. "Perhaps, gentlemen, we think that we are back in the days of the Reformation?" Then he did his roar again. "Singing? Dancing? Drinking?" He whirled his stick and cracked the tankard.

Virgilius stared into the tankard, and sighed. "Shweepstake tickets."

That sent the blood to Lispeen's forehead.

"I'll talk to you young bucks in the morning when I've had a word with your superior. Good evening to you."

The door slammed. We heard him go downstairs. His voice boomed in the kitchen at the Ryders. Then we saw his shadow passing across the paling sheen of the lake.

"The bosthoon," hissed Majellan.

"Jelly," moaned Virgilius, who had seized the situation at once, "we're for the long drop!"

With that we stole down the corridor and tapped at the sisters' doors and conferred in a huddle, and Virgilius and Chrysostom blamed Majellan for speaking back, but Magdalen said, "You were quite right, Brother. He is no gentleman." But Chrysostom kept pulling her fingers and looking at each of us in turn. She knew, too, how all this would appear back in the city, where the bishop and their superiors would say, "What is this! Nuns and monks living in the same house? Dancing together? Singing choruses? Playing pitch-and-toss out in the garden? And what's all this about *a tankard?*"

Magdalen said next morning that she heard Chrysostom crying late into the night.

Actually nothing at all happened. Old Ryder and the parish priest between them must have put a stop to the curate's gallop. After all, curates come and curates go but parish priests, like the brook, go on forever. But the story spread, and the students gathered around the four to comfort and encourage them, and of evenings people started to walk out to Ryder's and, in spite of Sister Chrysostom's warnings and tremors, we began to have regular concerts in the garden. The four even began to go out on surreptitious boating parties, and the bed-at-nine rule gradually became bed at ten, and even bed at eleven, until they were soon having as happy a time as anybody. Or should have, if their consciences were at ease. But were they? For, looking back at it now, I think I understand what had occurred. The Serpent had come into the garden with the most wily of temptations. He had said, "How dare you eat this apple?" And straightaway they began to eat it. They swallowed the last morsel of their apple the night before they were due to return to the city, perhaps for a lifetime, among the smelly slums about their schools.

We were moody that evening in the garden.

"I suppose this will be the last time we'll see the moon on the lake," said Sister Magdalen.

But the moon would not be up until after eleven, and a fairy wind in the reeds, ruffling the stars in the water into a fuzz, meant that even then there might be a clouded night.

"Our bus goes at seven," said Sister Chrysostom. "When does yours go, Brother Virgilius?"

By anticipation they were already becoming formal with one another.

"Half past seven," said Brother Virgilius.

"Who'll walk as far as the lake?" suggested Brother Majellan.

They went down the white road. Autumn was coming already. A white mist hung low over the river. The lake was breathed upon. They stood at the edge of it and looked at the low hills beyond.

"Sure, we can be looking forward to next year," said Brother Virgilius cheerfully.

"If there are any summer courses next year," murmured Sister Magdalen.

The soft sound of oars was heard and a boat appeared out on the water. The people in it were singing quietly; a last boating party. It was one of those big bargelike boats built for excursion parties, and there must have been twenty people in it, crushed shoulder to shoulder. Majellan hailed them and they approached and when they invited the four out for a row even Chrissy hardly demurred. The presence of the two monks and the two nuns seemed to cheer them up, for as they rowed away towards the narrows, making for the upper lake, the songs became louder and more merry. The lights of the village overflowed into the lake. Promenaders there heard them and sang back. Doubtless the curate heard them, too, and thanked God they would all be gone in the morning.

Time ceases to exist on a lake: every fisherman knows that. Somebody said that the moon would be up at eleven and would light them home. Chrissy whispered to Maggie that that would be very late, and what would happen if some message came from the hostel? But Maggie hushed her passionately, and Virgilius cried, "Let the last night be the longest."

It was much later than eleven before they got through the narrows – the old barge stuck there as it always did. Then the grey mountain slowly swelled up like a ghost against the spreading moon, and the whole land became black and white. On the bright side of the land the white cottages shone under their tarry roofs, and on the dark hills their scattered yellow lights invited us home. It became cold on the water. Rowing back against the current was a slow business. Heavy drops of phosphorescence fell from the blades. Presently a voice said, "It is near twelve, lads, put your backs into it." Now they were not singing at all; nor did they sing again until they saw the remaining village lights – only one or two left now. And they did not sing Irish songs, which are nearly all melancholy, but old music-hall songs like "Daisy, Daisy", and "The Girls You Can't Forget". The barge was not much more than twelve feet from the shore when they saw, clear in the moonlight, the black figure standing on the causeway. Majellan yelled, "Backwater!" The barge slewed around.

"I suppose, my dear ladies and gentlemen, that it does not matter to you that you are keeping the whole village awake?"

Nobody replied. The rowers set off for the opposite shore. The two brothers turned up their coat collars to hide their Roman collars. The two nuns hid their gimps and coifs with borrowed coats. Everybody was feeling cross and tired. As they neared the far shore the same black figure awaited them. He had raced round by the bridge, and gone leaping over heather and bog pool.

"You won't land here tonight until I have the name of every person on that boat!"

The midnight mountain cried back, "On – that – boat." The boat pushed off again and in mid-lake they held a conference: for even lay teachers do not like falling out with a priest. And the four religious? There was only one thing to do. It was easy to disguise Majellan and Virgilius: caps for black hats, and the Roman collars ripped off. The nuns had to remove gimps and cowls, put on kerchiefs and pin up their skirts. Then the boat again rowed to the landing place, the men crushed around the priest arguing loudly, and the rest ran. In five minutes he was alone on the causeway. At his feet he saw a white object on the stones: a nun's starched gimp. As he looked at it he trembled like a dog.

He was no longer alone by the moon-flooded lake. He was roaring in the pulpit, holding up the gimp: he was in the bishop's palace quietly unfolding a pale linen object out of brown paper: he was in the parish priest's sitting room and the white thing lay between them on the table: he was knocking at Ryder's door – yes, even if it was nearly one o'clock in the morning. He might have done all these things if, when he got back to his cottage, there had not been a sick call before him, and he had to get out his car and drive at once three and a half miles into the heart of the hills. Half an hour later he was tearing back. He had been hoaxed. The window of his cottage was open. The gimp was gone. It was the one good deed I did for my four friends.

I was awakened by the supernaturally bright light: it was not the sunrise, it was the sinking moon. My watch showed me that it was barely turned five o'clock. Dew and mist were all around the silent house: the lake was frosty; the sky pallid. The trees were weighted with sleep. Only the ceaseless mountain stream and the deceived birds made a sweet noise. Below in the garden, by the wooden gate, stood Majellan and Magdalen, talking . . .

I never saw Magdalen again; I never saw Virgilius again; I never saw Chrysostom again.

That was 1920, and not for twenty-three years did I meet Majellan. He was, of course, still a monk, and will always be: he was greying, and a little stooped, and much thinner. His eager, doggy eyes lit up for me: until I began to joke about those days, and then the light faded. I asked him about the others, and he told me that Virgilius was now a principal somewhere. He had not heard of the two nuns since that night on the lake.

"Ah!" I sighed. "Great days! But nobody wants to learn the language now. The mountains are empty."

"Yes. The mountains are empty."

"What a shame!"

"Mind you," he said, after a moment, "I'm not sure that I altogether approve of young people going out to these places. I hope I'm not being puritanical or anything like that, but . . . well, you know the sort of thing that goes on there."

I was so shocked that I could not reply for a moment.

"But, surely, it's all very harmless?"

He shook his head seriously.

"Maybe. You *never* know."

I said something idle. Then I asked him did he go out there at all nowadays.

"That was our last year."

"I hope it wasn't any trouble with your superiors?" I asked anxiously.

"Oh, nothing like that. No. It was just . . ." He looked away. Then he said over his shoulder, "I didn't much want to, really." Then he looked at me, and in a little gush of confidence he said, "You mightn't understand it, now! But it's not good to take people out of their rut. I didn't enjoy that summer."

I said I understood that. After a few more words, we parted. He smiled, said he was delighted to see I was looking so well, and went off, stooping his way back to his monastery in the slum.

By coincidence, two hours later, I found myself side by side with Lispeen, looking into a bookshop window. He was scarcely changed, except for a faint brush of grey at each ear; he wore a tall silk hat and carried a silver-headed umbrella. When I spoke to him and he turned, the sunset struck his rosy face and lit the sides of his hat so that they glowed and shone. With difficulty I brought his mind back to those years, but when I did he greeted me as heartily as if I was his best friend, and laughed so merrily at the memory of those old days that I almost expected him to clap me on the back.

"Of course, you know," he confided, with wide eyes, "they were only children. Such innocents!" He laughed at the thought of the innocents. "Of course, I *had* to frighten them!" And he laughed again, and then threw up his head and said "Heigh-ho" in a big sigh. Then he shook my hand, and beamed at me, told me I was looking grand, and went his cheerful way. He bowed benevolently to every respectful salute along the glowing street, and, when he did, his elongated shadow waved behind him like a tail.

Biographical Notes

Sean O'Faolain was born in Cork City in 1900, the son of a policeman in the Royal Irish Constabulary called Denis Whelan. He adopted the Irish form of his name when, at the age of 16, he developed an enthusiasm for Gaelic culture. In this he was influenced by one of his teachers who took part in the Easter Rising of 1916, and by his girl friend Eileen Gould (later his wife), who introduced him to the Irish-speaking areas of West Cork. In these years he became a close friend of Michael O'Donovan (Frank O'Connor), with whom he shared the same interests and enthusiasms.

As a student at University College, Cork he became involved with the Irish Volunteers (I.R.A.). In the Civil War which broke out after the 1920 Treaty, he and most of his friends took the Republican side. They were defeated and Eileen spent a year in prison. The ruthlessness of the victorious "Free Staters" in suppressing the opposition, and the opportunism of many defeated Republicans, caused O'Faolain to become disillusioned with politics, and he turned to an academic career – and to writing.

After graduating in Cork, he taught in a provincial town for a year, and then studied for three years at Harvard University. After some hesitation he and his wife made a conscious decision to return to Ireland, in spite of what they saw as the provincialism and bigotry of post-revolutionary Ireland. In the years to follow, O'Faolain wrote several novels, biographies, travel books and literary criticism, as well as several collections of short stories: the best of these stories combine sympathy for his characters with a strong personal indictment of the less attractive features of Irish society.

He became very influential in the 1940s as editor of a literary magazine, in which he gave encouragement to younger writers and fought against censorship and other forms of cultural repression. Due to the efforts of people like O'Faolain, the censorship laws were gradually repealed and a somewhat more liberal climate now prevails in Ireland. He now lives with his family near Dublin. His wife has published several books of Irish folk-tales, and his daughter is becoming well known as a writer of short stories and novels.

Annotations

5 **Sean** [ʃɔ:n] *Gael.* form of 'John' – **O'Faolain** [o:'fwe:lɑ:ɪn] – 1 **the mountains** *here:* the mountainous areas of the west where Irish is still spoken – 7 **utterly** completely – 8 **bog** area of land covered with turf – 9 **loch** [lox/lɒx] *Gael.* lake – 10 **file** line – 11 **scarp** steep hillside – 12 **to court** to go out with and express love to (a girl) – **bevy** group – **sedate** quiet and dignified – 13 **lay (men/women)** not members of a religious order (Most Irish secondary schools and large primary schools are run by religious orders. "Lay" teachers are employed by these orders, or run smaller country schools under the authority of a Parish Priest. All receive state salaries.) – 16 **accommodation** somewhere to stay – **to take lodgings** to stay (in a house, hotel, etc.) – 17 **derelict** ['– – –] old, in bad condition – 18 **landlords** owners of land which is rented – **the Revolution** *here:* the achievement of political independence from Britain – 19 **loft** part of a house under the roof – **dormitory** room in which a large number of people sleep – 20 **stifling** lacking in fresh air – 21 **rug** blanket – 23 **tick** little insect that digs into one's skin (Zecke) – 24 **to suffocate** to die from lack of air – 25 **baking** *here:* very hot – **slates** covering for a roof – 28 **to cajole** to persuade by talking in a friendly way

6 2 **dainty** very fine in appearance, movements, etc. – 3 **convent** house in which a community of nuns lives – 4 **Chrysostom** [–'– –] – **blotchy** uneven in colour – 5 **prim** very correct – 11 **hurler** man who plays the Gaelic game of hurling, which is somewhat similar to hockey – 12 **Majellan** [–'– –] – 13 **complexion** kind of skin – **beaming** *here:* smiling – 19 **drawing room** sitting room – 30 **cearrbhach** [ˌkja'ruwəx] *Gael.* – 33 **paws** feet of a cat, dog, etc.; *here:* hands – 36 **gambler** person who risks money on games of luck – 37 **guttural** ['gʌtərəl] with sounds made in the back of the throat – 38 **peruke** [pə'ru:k] wig

37 5 **shpit** *dial.* spit, saliva – 14 **peasant** small farmer, land worker – 19 **to retire** *here:* to go to bed – 22 **Saxon** *here:* English – 24 **wisp** small strand of s.th. (hair, etc.) – 31 **Do rugadh mé** [do 'rugəx me:] *Gael.* – **An Teampall Mór** [an 'tjampəl 'mo:r] *Gael.* – 38 **fuchsia** ['fju:ʃə] flowering bush which grows wild along the west coast

38 6 **Kilfinane** [kɪl'fɪnən] – 7 **thigh** upper part of the leg – 8 **yerrah, wisha** *Ir.* exclamations – 11 **Kilmallock** [–'– –] – 13 **rath** *Ir.* hill or mound associated with some legend; usually a burial place of archeological interest – 21 **six counties** probably Limerick, Cork, Waterford, Tipperary, Kerry and Clare – 31 **a lone child** an only child – 34 **to flit** to move very quickly – 36 **to dab** to wipe lightly with a cloth – 38 **to vaporize** *here:* to make seem hazy

39 1 **pitch and toss** a game played with coins – 9 **Bab Eró 'gus Ó mo mhíle Grá** ['bɑb ə'ro: gəs 'o: mo 'vi:lə grɑ:] *Gael.* (first three syllables meaningless) . . . and oh, my thousand-fold love – 25 **gom** *Ir. sl.* idiot – 27 **to bump against** to collide with – 30 **clout** slap – 32 **settle** long wooden seat – 38 **exuberant** very lively – **coarse** rough, not polite

40 1 **chewing the cud** chewing grass – 2 **tankard** large container for beer – 3 **tug of war** game in which two teams pull a rope opposite directions – 8 **curate** assistant priest in a parish (second only to Parish Priest in authority) – 9 **parish** area organized around a church – 10 **pompous** conscious and proud of one's importance – **cocksure** over-confident – 12 **cinema reel** part of a film – 13 **waxworks** stiff figures made of wax – 16 **postmistress** woman in charge of a post office – **office** *here:* special prayers said daily by a priest – 20 **caterwauling** unpleasant sounds like those made by cats at night – **Martin Luther** reference to the corruption in the Church against which M. L. protested – 21 **to stab** to point a stick at – 22 **coif** [kɔɪf] close head-covering worn by nuns – 26 **self-possessed** self-controlled and confident – 34 **to swell** to grow in size – 35 **to answer s.o. back** to contradict s.o. in authority – 36 **to hold one's ground** not to give in (in a conflict) – 40 **sure . . .** [ʃər] *Ir.* conjunction indicating mild opposition

41 1 **to gasp** to draw one's breath suddenly – 2 **elocution** the art of good, clear speech – 4 **shooting stick** stick with a surface for sitting on – **to teeter** to move from side to side unsteadily – 7 **to crack** *here:* to make a sharp noise on – 9 **sweepstake** lottery – **s(h)weepstake tickets** probably a demonstrative 'weakening' of a swear word such as "Sweet Jesus" – 11 **buck** frivolous young man – 12 **superior** *here:* head of the religious order – 15 **sheen** soft glow – 16 **the bosthoon** (= **bostún** *Gael.*) the bastard – 18 **the long drop** the hanging (exaggeration) – 29 **to put a stop to s.o.'s gallop** *Ir. coll.* to stop s.o.'s over-enthusiasm – 31 **the brook** reference to verse of a popular poem: "For men may come and men may go, but I go on forever" – 34 **tremor** shake – 35 **surreptitious** secret – 40 **Serpent** devil (as in Garden of Eden) – **wily** clever, cunning

42 2 **morsel** little piece – 5 **moody** feeling sad, irritable, etc. – 9 **reeds** grass-like plants growing in water – 13 **by anticipation** in expectation of s.th. – 24 **bargelike** long and flat, like a barge – 25 **to hail** to greet – 27 **to demur** to express unwillingness – 36 **to hush** [ʌ] to try make s.o. keep quiet – **passionately** with great feeling

43 2 **tarry** ['tɑ:rɪ] black, like tar – 4 **phosphorescence** [– –'– –] – 8 **melancholy** ['– – – –] – 12 **backwater** *here:* row backwards – **to slew around** to turn around – 17 **gimp** [g] stiff white cloth worn by nuns in front of their dresses – 19 **heather** [e] plant with purple or white flowers (Heidekraut, Erika) – 25 **to fall out with** to quarrel with, to break off a friendship – **religious** *here:* nuns and monks – 28 **cowl** hood-like head-covering worn by nuns – **kerchief** ['kɜ:tʃɪf] head-scarf – 30 **causeway** raised walk-way – 31 **starched** made stiff – 34 **pulpit** [ʊ] place in a church from which a priest gives a sermon – 35 **linen** ['lɪnən] – 39 **a sick call** a visit to a sick person

44 1 **to hoax** to trick – 7 **pallid** pale – 13 **1920** period after declaration of Irish independence, but before formal Treaty with Britain – 38 **rut** routine

45 1 **to stoop** *here:* to walk with one's head bent down – 17 **benevolent** kind, friendly, well-meaning

Interpretation and Teaching Notes

Background, Content and Analysis

"The Man Who Invented Sin" is the title story of Sean O'Faolain's third collection of short stories. This is the collection which, in the author's own account[1], marks his outgrowing of the romanticism of his youth, and his coming to terms with the realities of life in Ireland. In tone and in content, this story reflects one of the dominant themes of the author's middle and later years – his concern for the spiritual and cultural quality of life in the Republic he had fought to create.

As regards its form, it would be interesting to try to put it in one of the categories established by the author in his later theoretical writings:

> As I see it, a Short Story ... is like a child's kite, a small wonder, a brief, bright moment. It has its limitations ... It may not wander far ... it will only carry a few characters, ... there is not time, or space for elaborate characterization ... and there is often no plot, nothing much more than a situation, and only just enough of that to release a moment or two of drama, enough to let the wilful kite swirl ... A Short Story is concentrated stuff ... Maupassant and Chekhov invented it between them.
> A Tale is quite different. Like a small plane it is much more free, carries a bit more cargo, roves farther, has time and space for more complex characterization, more changes of mood, more incidents and scenes, even more plot.[2]

Though these categories are not mutually exclusive, most stories containing a mixture of the characteristics of both types, it is easy to see that "The Man who Invented Sin" is more of a "Tale" in the relaxed traditional mode than a "Short Story" as narrowly defined here.

It is organized in the form of a man's reminiscences of a summer course in the *Gaeltacht* ['geəltaxt] (Irish-speaking district) which he attended in his youth – presumably brought to his mind by the more recent incident with which the story ends. Between the opening line, which makes the narrative distance explicit, and the final incident, we therefore see the narrator as a young man. By and large, he restricts himself to relating his thoughts and feelings at the time; only occasionally are we reminded of the time that has elapsed between the action of the story and the telling of it. There is one

1 Cf. the author's Foreword to *Stories of Sean O'Faolain*; p. 11, Penguin edition.

2 Author's preface to *The Heat of the Sun*; p. 7, Penguin edition.

indication that he is no longer sure of all the details (p. 39, l. 1), which contributes to the plausibility of the tale: we are given the impression that the narrator is making an honest, though necessarily subjective effort to reconstruct the events of a summer twenty-three years ago. At another point in the narrative (p. 41, l. 39 – p. 42, l. 4) he pauses to reflect, with hindsight, on the significance of certain developments. Though this reflection is slightly redundant – something the author would have hardly allowed himself in one of his more concentrated "Short Stories" – it is appropriate to the 'reminiscing' which provides the framework of the story.

The narrator reveals himself to be a pleasant young man, probably a student or teacher (long holidays, desire to learn Irish), fun-loving and extrovert (cf. p. 39, ll. 34–38). There would be considerable justification for regarding him as a 'persona' of the author: not only are there several points of contact with O'Faolain's own background and development, but he is presented sympathetically from the start as a figure to identify with. In any case, the attitudes he represents and any opinions he expresses are fully in accordance with what emerges as the message of the story as a whole.

The narrator plays only a minor part in the action, which centres around his four fellow-students – two nuns and two monks who are forced, because of overcrowding in their respective hostels, to seek accommodation in the private house where he happens to be staying. Apart from a small number of contributions to the developments – which are, however, fairly decisive (p. 39, ll. 7–9; p. 41, ll. 19–20; p. 44, ll. 2–3) – he is mainly in the position of an observer-narrator.

What he observes is the gradual 'loosening-up' of his fellow-students when freed from the restrictive discipline of monastery and convent and forced by circumstances (and the weather, p. 36, ll. 22–28) into normal human contact with one another. At the beginning of this process, the two nuns, Sisters Chrysostom and Magdalen, are rather prim and reserved, though the latter reveals something of her spirited nature in occasional heated arguments with the more studious and intellectual of the two monks, Brother Majellan. The other monk, Brother Virgilius, is described as a simple countryman, and as such, is the least inhibited of the four in speech and manner. It is his child-like excitement at hearing that the prim Sister Chrysostom and himself come from neighbouring villages that breaks the ice, and they are soon playing pitch-and-toss, singing songs (under the narrator's tuition), and calling each other by their new nicknames, "Chrissy", "Maggie", "Jelly" and "Jilly" (p. 39, ll. 1–15).

All of this is still a very long way from the freedom enjoyed by the narrator, as suggested by his references in the first paragraph to dances, moonlight boating parties, "courting", the pub, bathing naked, etc. This contrast, underlined by the reference to the young man's late nights (p. 39, ll. 34–38), reminds us of the potential for conflict inherent in the situation. The closeness which seems to be developing (p. 39, ll. 30–38; p. 39, ll. 18–24) between Majellan and Magdalen points in the direction of one possible conflict with the ethos of the monastic way of life to which they are committed. But at this point, their discovery of the simple pleasures of life is totally innocent.

All this changes with the arrival on the scene of the local curate, a young priest seemingly anxious to impress his superiors, and known among the students by the derogatory nickname, "Lispeen". His display of moral indignation at finding monks and nuns dancing with each other and singing (p. 40, ll. 14–22) gives rise to a variety of reactions among the four culprits: Virgilius is intimidated, and Chrysostom is deeply upset (p. 41, ll. 27–28); Magdalen retains her dignity and self-possession, and the quiet Majellan becomes openly defiant, mainly in her defence. But in one respect, their reaction is identical. When it transpires that the parish priest has been persuaded to "put a stop to the curate's gallop" (p. 41, l. 30), the four start staying up late, going on surreptitious boating parties, and in general, enjoying themselves just like the other students. In retrospect, however, the narrator wonders whether they really were enjoying themselves (p. 41, l. 38 – p. 42, l. 4): "... I think I understand what had occurred. The Serpent had come into the garden with the most wily of temptations. He had said, 'How dare you eat this apple?' And straightaway they began to eat it. They swallowed the last morsel of their apple the night before they were due to return to the city, perhaps for a lifetime, among the smelly slums about their schools."

This insight has been forced on him by his meeting, twenty-three years later, with Brother Majellan. The monk's repudiation of his own behaviour that summer is expressed in terms which seem more appropriate to someone like Lispeen (p. 44, ll. 23–26): "I'm not sure that I altogether approve of young people going out to these places ... you know the sort of thing that goes on there." His revelation that he "didn't enjoy that summer" (ll. 38–39) suggests that he was bothered by feelings of guilt at the time. After the curate's rebuke, his behaviour had taken on the nature of deliberate defiance, i.e. 'sin'. We can assume that this is how he now sees his affection for Sister Magdalen (cf. ll. 4–10): his innocence and peace has been destroyed.

The man responsible for this (i.e. for 'inventing sin') is not troubled by any such qualms. When the narrator runs into him "by coincidence, two hours later" (p. 45, l. 3), the curate (presumably now a parish priest, to judge by his obvious prosperity and the respect accorded to him by the passers-by), talks in jovial tones of his role in the affair. He reveals himself as an opportunist who is totally impervious to the effects of his actions on other people.

In depicting the curate in this way, and in ending the story with the image of the curate's shadow, "waving behind him like a tail", O'Faolain undoubtedly intends an indirect comment on the influence of the Church on Irish life. One must remember that by the mid-forties, when this story was written, little was left of the cultural renaissance which accompanied the fight for independence. Books were being banned and writers and intellectuals forced to emigrate, all in the name of the dominant, narrowly Catholic view of what it meant to be Irish[3]. This deterioration is represented in the story by the contrast between the enthusiasm of the early days of the Republic and the materialism and neglect of traditions implicit in the narrator's remark: "... nobody wants to learn the language now. The mountains are empty" (p. 44, ll. 19–20). When one considers the massive presence of the Church in the field of education (cf. p. 35, ll. 13–15; p. 43, ll. 24–25), it does not seem unfair to attribute some of the blame to its influence.

It would be a mistake, however, to read an anti-Catholic message into the story. Not only did Sean O'Faolain (unlike Joyce) never reject Irish nationalism as such, but he also held on to his Catholic faith. Though he strongly objected to the anti-humanism of the Irish clergy, his travels abroad prevented him from attributing their faults to the religion as such. The following paradoxical statement sums up his attitude: "I was in fact exactly forty-six years old before I finally abandoned the faith of my fathers, and under the life-loving example of Italy, became converted to Roman Catholicism."[4]

In the context of the story, the kind of life-loving Catholicism which the author accepts is represented by the students, including the monks and nuns. The fact that it exists is, for the author, grounds for hope that it may one day come to prevail – grounds for his feeling (expressed in a comment on a different story) "that Ireland is not dead but sleeping"[5].

3 Cf. Sean O'Faolain, *The Irish*, pp. 109–121

4 From an article in the *Irish University Review*, Spring 1976; quoted by Guy Le Moigne in his essay on O'Faolain in *The Irish Short Story*, ed. Rafroidi

5 Author's Foreword to *Stories of Sean O'Faolain*; p. 11, Penguin edition

Additional Background Information

The folk-song referred to in the text (*Bab Eró,* normally written *Báboró*) is sung to the following air:

First Unit
The Narrator and the Narrative Situation

Preparation: The students should have read the whole story, at least in a cursory fashion.

1. Characteristics of the narrator
What impression do you get of the person who is telling the story?
A young man, most probably a student or young teacher, fun-loving, enjoys his holidays (a summer course in Irish in the mountains), sympathetic towards his fellow-students (esp. p. 35, ll. 1–15; p. 36, ll. 2–3, 14; p. 40, ll. 34–38; p. 45, ll. 2–3).

2. Point of view
How involved is the narrator in the story he is telling?
Quite closely involved in the events surrounding the monks and nuns, but plays only a minor part in the action (e.g. p. 39, ll. 7–9; p. 41, ll. 19–20; p. 44, ll. 2–3); mainly in the role of an observer-narrator.
Is the information he gives appropriate to his position in the story?
Point of view limited to what he saw and heard, and to what he himself did and thought. Only exception: p. 43, ll. 33–37, where he imaginatively pretends to know what the curate's feelings were.

3. Narrative distance
Where does it become clear from what point in time the story is being told?
Opening line indicates that he is telling the story later in life; reminder on p. 41, l. 39; more precise indication of time distance on p. 44, l. 13, as introduction to a final episode which, we assume, is close to the time of the telling of the story.

How does this time difference influence his viewpoint?
The narrative distance allows him to reflect on the significance of certain developments (p. 41, l. 39 – p. 42, l. 4); but it also means he cannot be sure of all the details, e.g. "I think it was Virgilius ..." (p. 39, l. 1). We get the impression of an honest, though subjective attempt to reconstruct the events of a summer twenty-three years ago.

Homework: Write a short character sketch of one of the monks or nuns. [Allow students to choose, but ensure equal distribution.]

Second Unit
The Characters and Their Development

1. Direct characterization
How does the narrator describe the two nuns and the two monks? (Mainly page 36)
Sister Magdalen – dainty, gay, spirited, a shame to lock away in a convent, a city girl, ladylike (the latter a remark by Brother Virgilius, p. 37, l. 1).
Sister Chrysostom – tall, delicate, big hands and blotchy skin, a bit prim.
Brother Virgilius – a country man, big and strong, no nerves, a powerful voice, a fine hurler, natural ways.
Brother Majellan – gentle, rosy cheeks, soft complexion, beaming eyes, wears glasses, intelligent, sensitive, earnest.

2. Indirect characterization
How much of this is borne out by what they actually say and do at the beginning of the story?
Magdalen – her "dainty", urban pronunciation of Irish (p. 36, l. 37 – p. 37, l. 3); spirited arguments with Majellan (p. 37, ll. 13–18).
Chrysostom – her prim rebuke of Virgilius (ll. 8–9, similarly l. 19).
Virgilius – his uninhibited hilarity (p. 36, ll. 33–36); his demonstratively unrefined, country pronunciation (p. 37, l. 5), his dislike of arguments (ll. 15–16).
Majellan – the earnestness of his remarks, heated arguments (p. 36. ll. 29–30; p. 37, ll. 10–11).

3. The basic conflict
Examine the opening paragraph of the story. What does it suggest about the situation the monks and nuns find themselves in?
Topic: gaiety in the summer holidays; the pleasures the narrator enjoys –

dances, moonlight boating parties, sing-songs, the pub, bathing naked, 'courting', etc. – are for the most part forbidden to his fellow-students.

4. The development of the four students up to the end of the summer.
To what extent do the four change in the course of the story?
All free themselves from certain inhibitions and reveal hidden sides to their characters:
Magdalen becomes the most fun-loving of the lot, more spirited than was evident at the beginning, grows fond of Majellan (p. 38, ll. 35–37; p. 39, ll. 21–23; p. 40, l. 3, 25–30; p. 41, ll. 21–22; p. 42, ll. 36–37).
Chrysostom shows what a good singer she is, loses some of her primness, comes to enjoy the fun, but remains rather timid and reveals how vulnerable and easily hurt she is (p. 38, ll. 10–24; p. 39, ll. 10–13; p. 40, ll. 4–5, 21–23; p. 41, ll. 20–23, 27–28, 34; p. 42, l. 37).
Virgilius changes least, as he was rather irreverent to begin with; his behaviour becomes less monk-like, but he also reveals that he is more easily intimidated than the quieter Majellan (p. 38, l. 7; p. 39, l. 1; p. 40, ll. 1–3, 38–39; p. 41, l. 7, 17–18).
Majellan's earnestness turns into affection for Magdalen, and he becomes very defiant, mainly in her defence (p. 40, ll. 3, 27–37, p. 41, l. 16).

5. Their (probable) fate
How much are we told about what happened to them afterwards?
Explicit information only about Majellan: he has reverted to 'normal' monastic life, and regrets the episode in the mountains. We can assume that the fate of the others was somewhat similar.

Homework: Re-read the story, paying particular attention to the role of the curate.

Third Unit
The Curate's Shadow

1. The curate's motivation
What is said or suggested in the story about the position of parish priest and curate in an Irish village?
Both respected – or even feared – as figures of authority (p. 40, ll. 32, 38–39); this is reflected in the reactions of the nuns and monks – and even the attitude of the "lay teachers" (p. 43, ll. 24–25). No reasons are given for such unquestioning acceptance of their authority, except for oblique refer-

ences to massive Church presence in the field of education (p. 35, ll. 13–18). A curate is subordinate to a parish priest (p. 41, ll. 29–31) and frequently changes parishes until he is finally allocated a parish of his own.
How does 'Lispeen' fit into this power structure?
Characterized as young, arrogant, and eager to impress his superiors – especially the bishop (p. 40, ll. 8–11; p. 43, ll. 30–37); probably anxious to be promoted to parish priest; his apparent 'change of heart' at the end of the story suggests he has achieved his ambition.

2. The narrator's later encounter with Lispeen and Majellan
What is surprising about the attitudes expressed by Majellan and Lispeen twenty-three years later?
Both seem to be reversals of what they stood for in 1920. Majellan, who had appeared to be innocently and uninhibitedly enjoying himself, now claims that this was not so; he expresses opinions that would seem more appropriate to Lispeen. Lispeen, on the other hand, claims to have been only playing a role, and laughs at the memory.

3. The significance of the title
Who can be said to have "invented sin"? – And what has this got to do with Majellan's surprising revelation?
The curate's rebuke (p. 40, l. 14 – p. 41, l. 12) destroys the four students' innocence and peace; from then on, their participation in late-night boating parties, etc. takes on the nature of deliberate defiance, i.e. in their Catholic consciousness, 'sin'. This would also apply to the affection felt by Magdalen and Majellan for one another (cf. p. 44, ll. 4–10). Majellan's revelation twenty-three years later suggests that he was bothered by feelings of guilt at the time. The narrator's explicit comparison of Lispeen with Satan in the Garden of Paradise (p. 41, l. 38 – p. 42, l. 4) is echoed at the end of the story in his reference to the curate's "elongated shadow ... like a tail".

4. Implicit social criticism
What impression does the final episode give of life in Ireland in the 1940s as opposed to the early 1920s?
The contrast with the enthusiasm of the early days of the Republic gives a negative impression of Irish life in the 1940s; explicit reference to the neglect of traditional culture (p. 44, ll. 19–22), which suggests materialism and forgetfulness of the ideals of the 'Revolution'; implicit negative view of the effect of the Church on Irish life, as represented by the curate's "elongated shadow". Note in particular his obvious prosperity, and the respect accorded to him as he walks away down the street.

For Further Study

Points for discussion

1. Pick out the references to landscape and the weather. Examine the imagery used, and the effects achieved by such descriptive passages.
2. What is the significance of the various references to the Irish language?
3. Compare the role of the curate in this story with that of Father Butler in Joyce's "An Encounter".

Courses/Projects based on this story

1. Stories by Sean O'Faolain
"The Man Who Invented Sin" plus a selection of the following, all except the last from *Stories of Sean O'Faolain* (Penguin, 1970):
- "The Trout" – also included in *Irish Short Stories* (Schöningh) and *Contemporary British Short Stories I* (CVK)
- "The End of a Good Man" – also in *Irish Short Stories* (Longman Imprint)
- "Lord and Master"
- "One True Friend" – simplified version in *One True Friend and Other Irish Short Stories* (Longman Structural Reader)
- "The Heat of the Sun" – from the collection of the same title (Pan paperback)

2. The Irish Republic: Ideal and Reality
- "The Man Who Invented Sin"
- Topical Texts 16: *Ireland and its Problems* (Klett), Chapter I – at least texts 1 and 2 (both from *The Irish* by Sean O'Faolain, Penguin 1969), 4, 5, 6, 7, 9
- From *Ireland: History and Present State,* (Diesterweg), "The Stuffed Shirts" by Sean O'Faolain (first published in the literary magazine *The Bell,* 1943)
- From the Klett slide series *Dias zur Landeskunde* (Ireland: 56815; Lehrerheft: 5681), the slides 2, 3, 13, 23–26

Mary Lavin

A Cup of Tea

"She'll take a cup of tea, no matter how late it is when she gets here. You can leave the kettle at the back of the stove where it will keep the heat without spilling over and putting out the fire."

"All right, ma'am," said the servant girl, and she threw a baleful glance at a picture of Sophy, for whom all this trouble was being taken, and who had been expected since early morning and would, as likely as not, arrive in the middle of the night, and get them all up out of their beds. The young servant's back was nearly broken from all the work that had been done in the last few days. They had scrubbed every floor in the house, cleaned all the windows, and they had gone as far as waxing Sophy's room twice in the one day because Sophy's mother had marked it so much with tracks of her feet going in and out with clean curtains and extra pillows, bunches of flowers and hot jars.

"She needs a holiday after all the hard work she has done," said her mother as she pushed the kettle further back on the stove, and then changed her mind and left it where it had been.

"I hope she'll pass her examination," said the servant, raising up from the floor in the hope of gaining a moment's rest by introducing a topic upon which her mistress always showed weakness and garrulity.

"Her examination!"

It was almost as if Sophy's mother had forgotten that Sophy had done any examination at all, so absorbed was she in the thought that her only daughter was coming home again after a three months' absence.

"Oh, her examination!" she repeated carelessly as her eyes ran over the tray that was already set for Sophy's breakfast in bed next morning. "Why, of course she'll pass. I expect she'll do very well, and get very good marks."

"She's very clever, isn't she?" said the young girl, in a tone of voice in which she was careful to mingle mixed ingredients of envy and flattery, as a good farmer mingles his grasses with cocksfoot and ratstail and clover when he lays down a field.

"Oh, she has a good brain, I suppose," said Sophy's mother, in an offhand manner that so far from deceiving the servant, emboldened her to sit back on her hunkers and rest her limbs more freely.

"Why wouldn't she have brains!" said the young girl, "I suppose she takes after her father!" And jerking her finger and thumb she was about to point in dumb show at the ceiling, for over their head was the study in which Sophy's father was buried in books and lost in the fumes of tobacco smoke. He was an amateur entomologist.

But Sophy's mother turned around sharply.

"What time do you expect to get that floor scoured? Do you expect to be at it all night, or why are you sitting back and taking your ease like that?"

The girl grabbed the scouring brush again and began to rub it hastily on the big bar of soap that she had held indifferently in her hand while she had taken her ease.

Except for the noise of the rough brush going over the flagged floor there was no sound then for a few minutes, but it was clear from the expression upon her face that Sophy's mother was still brooding on what the servant had said.

"There's a great deal of difference between a hobby and a degree from a University!" she said at last, "and Sophy has done one of the hardest degrees in the University. There were only two girls in the Political Economy class, and only one in the class for the Study of International Relations." She smiled. "Her father spends a lot of his time up there in his study with his books and his collection-cases, but I hardly think that he'd make much out of Sophy's books! Did you ever see them? I never saw such books. So heavy! And figures and diagrams on every second page."

During this speech the mother's face relaxed somewhat and assumed an expression of satisfaction such as it had worn after Sophy's floor had been waxed the second time. "Of course, my husband is a great authority on insects," she said, grudgingly, as one who having very little respect for the position of another is nevertheless aware that upon the respect in which it is held by others his own importance depends. She was going to say something else, but just then the young servant ran to the window and began to pull off her apron and struggle to get it over her head.

"She's here! She's here!" cried the girl excitedly. And then, before the mother was into the living room and only half-way across the floor to the hallway, Sophy was running across the room to meet her, throwing her bag and scarf to either side of her, and putting out her arms to hug her mother with such a rattle of bracelets and metal buttons that although the cheeks that pressed against hers were soft and firm as plums and peaches her mother was reminded for a moment of Sophy's father and the way his watch-chain used to rattle against the buttons on his waistcoat long ago when he gave her a salutation. That was before he took to wearing smoking jackets with buttons of braid or velvet, and gave up bothering to carry around a watch of any kind. But the impression only lasted a moment.

"Stand back from me," she cried. "Let me look at you! You look thin. I hope you're not trying to slim yourself. How did the car drive up without my hearing it? Did you have a tiresome journey? What time did you leave? I hope you stopped on the road for a rest!"

The mother's eyes flew from Sophy's face to her waist, from her waist to her hair, and from her hair to her hands with that confused, distracted, and haphazard curiosity of love that is so different from the steady gaze of a stranger.

"How did you get on at your examination?" she asked, and then before Sophy had time to answer even the last of the questions, her mother threw up her hands. "Hold up your head! Don't stir!" she said, and she moved back as one moves back from a canvas at a picture gallery, the better to see it. "You're too thin," she said. "It doesn't suit you. It throws up your likeness to your father. I often heard people drawing attention to it, but I could never see it myself. But I see it now! I'd swear I was looking at him, except for his moustaches. How odd I never saw it before. Sometimes, I thought there was a slight resemblance in the way you turned your head, but only at certain times, if you were upset or annoyed about something. I can't say it was ever anything definite. It was nothing at all like the way you resemble my own sisters in your walk and the way you hold yourself. But I suppose it's natural that you should resemble him in something. It's a good thing you didn't inherit his disposition!"

As she made the last remark she felt Sophy draw away her hand, which she had still kept clasped in hers while leaning back to scrutinize her. Instantly she regretted having let her tongue run away with her, but Sophy's face gave no sign of annoyance. She had released her hands, certainly, but she had smiled as she moved away and began to gather up her scarf, her bag and her gloves. Still her mother regretted the remark.

"How is he?" said the girl, and then suddenly she sank down into an armchair in case her mother might think for a moment that she was impatient to go up to him.

"You'll have to go up and see him. He musn't have heard the car!" said her mother grudgingly, and then before she could stop herself she had given in to her spite again. "I don't know why he didn't hear the car! His study is to the side of the house, and I was in the kitchen, away at the back!" But almost at once, she made an effort to undo the harm she had done. "You had better run up and see him before you take off your hat and coat," she said, and then she urged herself to be even more pressing. "Please, dear!" she said, briskly. "Don't sit down until you have gone up to him, if only for a minute. You need only say a few words; just to please him. There's no need to stay. Just a few words! Don't sit down till you do it. If you sit down you won't feel like getting up." She walked over and taking her daughter's arm urged her to stand up by pressing her arm. "I'll have your cases brought up to your room while you're gone, and when you come down we'll have a nice chat. I want to hear all you have to tell me. But not until you come down again!"

Sophy began to get up from the armchair slowly. She pouted and put on an air of unwillingness, feeling compelled by an impulse of pity and compassion to play up to the pretence of her own reluctance with which her mother was deluding herself.

"Hurry, dear! You'll be glad you went. Just tell him you got here safely. He'd feel so hurt if you didn't go up."

"Why didn't he come down?" said Sophy, with a good appearance of resentment.

"He's coming to the final chapters of his work on those disgusting beetles he has all over the house," said her mother, and she shuddered. "He comes down for his meals because I insist, but he doesn't come down at all in the evenings. I see his light burning till all hours in the night. I say the book will want to bring in queer profits before it pays for all the lamp-oil he's burned in the last five years! Although who's going to buy it is more than I can make out unless there are more than I think of dried-up unnatural people like himself, that see more value in a bee's foot than they see in the company of the human beings around them!" Again she recollected herself quickly and rushed on without drawing a breath. "But go up," she cried. "Go to the door for a minute, anyway. There's no need to stay."

But as Sophy went out of the room dragging her feet, the mother knew in her heart that the girl would not come down again until she had to be called, and perhaps called more than once. Even as she listened she heard the footsteps getting faster. They stopped dragging and soon broke into a run, taking the stairs two at a time. Suddenly she thought of the lassitude and disinclination that Sophy had shown about going upstairs, although she had been as fresh as a daisy when she first came in, and seemed to freshen up quickly enough when she got to the stairs. Had she too been pretending? And why? Her mother regretted her own polite pretence, and almost ran out into the hallway to shout up the stairs, "Go on! Don't let me keep you. Go on. Run up to your father. Tell him all your news. Don't think of me. Don't tell me anything at all."

But she shut her mouth tightly and went out to tell the maid that she could go to bed, there was nothing more to be done.

The maid was worn out. She sat on a chair in front of the range with her legs apart and her head bent as she tried to take a splinter out of her thumb by sucking it.

"What is the matter? Is your finger sore? Put a poultice of bread and water on it and leave it on till morning." She looked around the kitchen. "You can go to bed now," she said, and then she remembered the bags. "You can carry up the baggage to her room before you go," she said, and then she went over to the pantry door. "Did you leave out a jug of milk?" she asked, "and a bowl of sugar? I forgot to ask her if she'd have a cup of tea, but I'm sure she'll want one."

The girl rose up unsteadily to her feet and went into the pantry. She came out with a large jug of milk, but her face had a dubious expression, and when she came into the light of the kitchen she put the jug to her nose and smelled it, making a grimace as she did so.

"Don't do that," shouted her mistress, nearly causing the girl to drop the jug. "Where did you pick up that disgusting habit?"

"I only wanted to see if the milk was sour. How could I find out without smelling it?" said the girl, not fully aware of the error of what she had done, but painfully aware of the error of having been seen doing it.

"The milk couldn't be sour. It's the afternoon's milk. Give it to me!"

"All the same," said the girl, and she handed over the jug, looking with interest to see in what superior way its condition would be tested by her mistress.

Sophy's mother took the jug and for a minute she seemed to hesitate, then she began to move it deliberately round and round in concentric circles a long way from her nose, but presumably within the orbit of her olfactory organs, for as she did so she sniffed two or three times. But the presumption was wrong.

"There is no need to stick your nose right into the jug," she said then, feeling a need to modify her former remarks on the subject, as she raised the jug and brought it slightly nearer to her nose, before she circled it round once more. This time her nostrils dilated slightly. The young girl tossed her head and took out a hair-slide rather unnecessarily since she fastened it in her hair again a minute later in the exact same place where it had been before. "Don't put your hands to your hair in the kitchen," said her lady absentmindedly, but she was looking around the kitchen. "Where is the small saucepan?" she said. "Oh, there it is. Rinse it out with clean water for me. And then you can go to bed. This milk is perfectly fresh, but it will do it no harm to give it a boil. That will make sure of it for the morning. It will be cool before Sophy comes downstairs, I'm sure."

The milk was well cooled when Sophy came down. Her mother had been up and down to her own room two or three times and had at last undressed and put on her slippers and dressing-gown. She walked heavily each time she passed her husband's study, but the talk and laughing inside may have prevented her footsteps from being heard. When she passed the boxroom under the stairs she heard the young servant snoring and groaning in her sleep.

"Oh Mother! I kept you up," cried Sophy when she came down at last and saw the slippers and dressing-gown. "Why did you wait up? Why didn't you call me?" And then, as if answering both of her own questions, she summed up the situation. "You should have gone to bed," she said.

"I thought you might like some tea," said her mother. "I kept the fire in. It was nearly out, but I was just in time to throw on a few logs."

"Oh good!" said Sophy.

Her mother's spirits that had sunk in the last hour began to rise again.

"I have the tray set," she said, "and I'll have a cup with you. I never take tea at this hour because it keeps me awake but I'll be awake tonight anyway, with excitement!"

Her spirits rose higher. She forgot her hurt at the hour Sophy had spent upstairs.

"I want to hear everything that happened since you went away. Begin at the beginning. Were you wet when you reached the station going back last time? I worried all night thinking of the long journey you had sitting in that cold railway carriage. They should have proper heating apparatus. It's disgraceful. Did you meet anyone going up in the train? Were you back on the right day? Were there any new people in your class?"

"I'm sure I told you all that in a letter," said Sophy, taken aback at her mother's accurate memory of a day she had difficulty in recalling.

"I could hear it a dozen times," said her mother. "Tell me everything!"

"Oh, there's nothing unusual to tell," said Sophy taking up a biscuit and beginning to chew it.

"You found plenty to tell your father it seems, judging by the length of time you stayed up with him," said her mother irritably.

Sophy looked up. "Oh, we were only talking," she said vaguely, for she could not, in fact, remember much of the lazy banter that she and her father exchanged when they met. "There's nothing much to tell. The exams were not too bad. The results will be in the paper." She paused and tried to remember something else to tell. "The second paper on the first day was a bit hard, but I think I'll pull through all right."

"I can hardly believe it's your final examination," said her mother. "How time flies! I lie awake nights wondering if we did right in sending you to the University. It puts such a strain on a girl. I hope you'll stay home for a while, even after the results come out. Indeed, if you like I'll speak to your father about letting you stay home entirely. It's very nice to have a degree and feel independent, but there's no need to carry things too far and wear yourself out working when your father himself makes no attempts to add to his income, although he could earn more than any man in the town if he wasn't so odd!"

"You have the wrong idea, Mother. I had a definite idea in taking out my degree."

The mother looked at her, at her glossy silk knees and her nice straight hair.

"Have you some plans?" she asked excitedly. "I'm so happy to have you home. Tell me your plans. I want to hear them. I want to help."

She remembered the way she went into her own mother's room years ago to sit in an armchair and brush her hair when she came back from a visit to a relation, telling her mother all about the dances to which she had gone, the partners with whom she had danced, about the underlinen her cousins had worn, the needlework they were doing, and even arranging her hair in the manner in which they had worn theirs so that nothing would be unknown to those at home of the way her time had been spent during her absence from them.

"One thing is certain," she said suddenly, speaking out of a dream. "You have my mother's hands. I never saw anything so remarkable. She would have been so pleased to know it, but I never thought of telling her." She sighed and her faint sigh seemed to fill the air with ghostly memories and regrets, and Sophy moved in her chair, and stared down at her hands self-consciously, but seeing a loosened piece of cuticle on the forefinger of her left hand she became absorbed at once in trying to tear it off with the finger and thumb of her right hand, which she crooked to form a pincers. She gave two or three sharp tugs to the loose piece of skin but failed to tear it off each time. "Don't do that," said her mother. "It will be sore all night. It will keep you awake."

"I can't leave it alone," said Sophy, tugging at it again.

"You can. Forget about it. Stop looking at it. Tell me more about your examination. Tell me about your friends and you'll forget all about it, and it will knit back into the skin."

But Sophy could not forget the dead cuticle. It irritated her, and she kept at it. The mother spoke again in a dreamy voice.

"Poor Mother's hands were all blackened and hardened from work, but she wouldn't have grudged you your easy life. She would have been the first to congratulate you on your independence in going to the University. How it would have amused her to see your hands so much like her own. I wish I had thought of telling her. It's only when people are gone from us that we remember all the little things we could have done to please them!"

"Ah!" said Sophy. She had torn off the cuticle and she put her finger up to her mouth to ease the sting of the pain. Then she looked around at the tray. "How about the tea?" she said.

"The kettle is at the back of the stove," said her mother. "It will be almost boiling. I'll go out and get it. If we poke up the fire here it will bring the water to the boil in a minute."

"Is there any use bringing up tea to Father?" said Sophy when her mother came back into the room with the kettle.

"You can if you like," said the woman bending down to settle the kettle on the crackling logs in the grate. "I know the reception I'd get if I interrupted him at his work! Anyone would imagine it was for my own good I went up to him, to hear the way he turned on me upon the few occasions I was unwise enough to enquire if he'd like anything before I went to bed!"

"Oh, I'm so hungry! I'm so thirsty!" said Sophy, breaking in upon her mother urgently. "All the way down in the train I was thinking of those dear old cups with the impossible birds on them." She held up one of the frail cups and stared at its hand-painted rim. But her mother understood the interruption and flushed.

"If that's the case it's a wonder you stayed upstairs so long," she said bitterly, and once again, incongruously, she remembered the confidences that used to be exchanged between her own mother and herself long ago. It would have been such a relief, just once, to tell Sophy of some of the unpleasant things she had had to put up with while she was away. But Sophy was talking about the stupid old cups as if she wanted to stave off any chance of confidences. She was holding the cup in front of her with both hands and staring at it with burning cheeks and bright eyes. How could she be so excited about an old cup that she had seen in the china closet ever since she was able to toddle!

"Is it meant to be a real bird?" Sophy cried. "Is it a peacock? Is it a nightingale? Whoever saw such feathers! Whoever saw such colours!" Her voice was feverish and she asked question after question, laughing nervously at the same time. But in her heart she was trying to form some sort of a prayer. "Dear God, keep her from complaining about Father! I want to comfort her. I want to be understanding. I want to make her happy on my first night home. But I can't see things from her point of view. I can't see things from her point of view."

"Give me the cup," said her mother. "The tea is ready." She caught the small cup almost roughly. She disliked it with a sudden passion and could have thrown it on the floor only it was belonging to a set. Instead, she began to talk as normally as she could. "I'm looking forward to a cup of tea myself," she said. "Indeed, I'd take a cup every night if I had someone to take one with me. I used to love a cup at this hour. I don't know why I gave it up. You give up a great many things, one after another, when you are alone. Of course, I don't want company. I have my reading! I have my knitting! I have a big basket of socks to darn. It never seems to be empty!"

Poor Mother. Sophy looked at her mother's face as it was bent over the fire and for a moment she envied the fine structure of bone that made the face so clear and attractive in spite of age, and she looked at the grey hair that was still so full of life that it sprang into curling tendrils whenever it escaped from the combs that held it. She thought of her own large pale face and straight hair that gave her a resemblance to her father that in spite of her mother's difficulty in seeing it, she herself knew to be evident.

"The kettle is beginning to sing," said her mother, just then. "It's a good thing someone in the house has the heart to sing, as I often say to the maid, when your father has been particularly trying."

Sophy looked around quickly for something with which she could attract her mother's attention away from the abyss over which she trembled again. Her eyes fell on the old album, that her mother had taken from her old home, when she had left to get married. It was covered in faded blue velvet, with a large silver clasp.

"Did you paste in the picture of my class that I sent you at midterm?" she asked, and she leaned forward and took the album on her knee. It fell open at the page upon which she had gazed so frequently as a child, and which she had probably strained from the binding by the many times she leaned her elbows on the book to gaze better at the familiar picture. It was a photograph of her grandmother sitting in a wicker chair against a photographer's scenic screen of palms and clouds and trellis balustrades, and around her, grouped in formal postures, were her daughters, Sophy's mother, and Sophy's mother's sisters. And they all wore long white dresses with long white sleeves and high necks and white hats that tilted under the weight of floppy silk roses. They all wore gold brooches, and gold bracelets, and they all had great masses of nut-brown hair. And they sat with their arms entwined around each other's waists, while those of them nearest to the chair upon which their mother sat, leaned back against her or looked up into her face. Sophy always paused a moment before she picked out her own mother from the group of charming girls. She remembered that her mother often told her that it took the photographer twenty minutes to try and pose them, spreading out his hands, and exclaiming in Italian, and entreating them to stop laughing just for one minute. And all at once she remembered the other stories her mother used to tell her too, when she was a little girl and easily pleased, the stories of beaux and bouquets, and the stories of larks and pranks that were played upon everyone; the singing, and laughing, and the playing upon the piano that had gone on all day long. And she tried to feel sorry for her mother, all alone now, sitting here in the evenings filled with bitterness of those unfulfilled and foolish dreams.

But instead of a feeling of pity, Sophy felt an impatience and irritability – why did she marry the wrong man? But then another question formed itself in her mind as an answer to the first. Is it possible to be certain before it is too late that the man you are going to marry is the right man or not? But she was tired, and tiredness confused her mind, and she put both questions aside unanswered. Times have changed, she told herself easily. Women know more about men now than they did long ago. Marriages may break asunder nowadays, but they don't rot slowly.

"I hope you haven't given up sugar?" her mother asked. "It's so foolish of girls to try and be thinner than Nature intended them to be."

"Oh, I take sugar all right," said Sophy – and then she could not resist a slight protest. "I'm glad I take it because if I didn't I should hate to have you try and force me to do so, Mother!"

"Am I a scold?" said her mother, smiling and seeming to enjoy the idea as a joke. She passed the jug of milk. "Put in the milk yourself. You say I always give you too much."

But Sophy was staring into the jug.

"What is the matter with the milk?" she said, and she held it up to her nose.

"There's nothing the matter with it," said her mother, anxiously looking at her.

"Ugh!" said Sophy. "There's a scum on it! Ugh, it's disgusting! What is it?"

"Oh!" said her mother relaxing in relief. "I forgot to take off the scum. But it's nothing. It's quite all right. I just gave the milk a boil while you were upstairs. It wasn't sour, but it seemed on the point of turning. Boiling saves it, but it doesn't make any difference to the milk. You wouldn't notice any taste when it's in the tea. But I shouldn't have left the scum on it. That was stupid of me!" And she dragged off the scum with the back of a spoon. It crumpled up on the side of the jug like a piece of white silk. "There's nothing disgusting about it at all!" she said again, as she saw her daughter's grimace.

"Boiled milk gives a taste to the tea," said Sophy.

"Not at all," said her mother, pouring out a cup. "I often give it a boil at night."

"Is there any milk in the kitchen that has not been boiled?" said Sophy, drawing her empty cup away as her mother went to pour the tea into it. She stood up with the cup in her hand.

"I'm afraid not," said her mother, "but I assure you this is quite all right. You won't notice the difference when it's in the tea! I promise you. I wouldn't have done it otherwise. I'm too particular about things!"

Sophy sat down and held out the cup. When it was filled she raised it to her lips and sipped at it.

"I taste it distinctly!" she said, lowering the cup again.

"You couldn't, dear." Her mother sipped hers. "I don't taste it."

"Well I do," said Sophy, "and what's more, I can't drink the tea."

"But that's absurd," cried her mother. "It's just your imagination."

"It's not imagination. I think you might have left a little milk without being boiled, when you know a cup of tea means so much to me after a long journey."

"I tell you it makes absolutely no difference."

"Oh Mother! Let's not argue about it. I can't drink the tea; that's all! Oh, why did you boil it?"

The mother sat looking at her own tea, for which she too had suddenly a great distaste. Why did she boil the milk? She tried to remember. It wasn't sour. And even if it was beginning to turn it would have kept until Sophy had come down; a matter of thirty or forty minutes. Suddenly she remembered the way she had walked from room to room during those minutes, moving the kettle, stirring the fire, and filling in the time with aimless actions.

"Perhaps if you hadn't stayed so long upstairs I might not have had time to boil it!" she said, flinging out the excuse without caring what effect it had. The evening was spoiled, anyway. The whole week of work and preparation was spoiled too. Everything was spoiled.

Sophy got up from her chair. And now she looked very tired indeed. There was no mistaking the heavy black lines und her eyes and the way her mouth dropped at the sides.

"Don't harp on it, Mother," she said, and she thought to herself that this was the way her father and mother acted when she was out of earshot.

"That's right!" said her mother. "Lose your temper now! Go upstairs and bang your door! After all the trouble I took preparing for you this is all the thanks I get. It's good that I'm used to this kind of thing from your father!"

"Leave Father out of it!" cried Sophy.

"Two of a feather!" cried her mother.

Sophy threw out her hands in an appeal.

"I wish you wouldn't take it this way, Mother!"

"What other way can I take it?"

"You could admit that you made a mistake in boiling the milk without finding out whether I minded or not."

"I can't see now or then why you did mind it," said her mother. "It makes no difference whatever to the taste of the tea. At home we always gave milk a boil after supper to keep it from getting sour overnight."

"I never heard of it being done anywhere else," said Sophy. "You did a lot of things at home that sound queer to me, if it comes to that!"

Her mother drew in a quick breath.

"I suppose you heard your father say that! He's always having a slap at my sisters!"

"He never even mentions them, if you want to know!"

"Oh, that doesn't deceive me. There are more ways of sneering than by word of mouth. And indeed, now that we're mentioning such things, let me tell you that your own attitude isn't what it might be at times. When the old cock crows, the young cock cackles."

"Well, I can't help it, can I, if I'm like him?" said Sophy.

"There's no need to copy his ignorant traits," said her mother.

Sophy stuck her fingers into her ears.

"I won't listen to talk like that," she cried. "It's unjust. I never knew him to say or do anything that wasn't just as it should be!"

"Maybe if you were at home a little more you might not have the same thing to say for very long."

Sophy sprang to the door. "I must say I'm glad I don't come home very often if this is the kind of reception I get! Good night!" And she banged the door.

Sophy went up to the bedroom where the floor had been waxed twice over, and where the stiff muslin curtains floated back and forth as the winds urged them.

As she undressed she thought of the girls in the white dresses who vexed the photographer by laughing so much he could not pose them properly and she thought of the photograph of her father that hung in the hall, showing a stiff and straight young man with a broad face and serious eyes with a stern look in them. And suddenly she ran to her case and opened it, tossing up her blouses and handkerchiefs as she ran her hand to the bottom and took out a small photograph in a small frame. It was a photograph of another young man, also straight and also stiff, with serious eyes and a stern look, because these are the attributes which young men wish to appear to possess when they have their photographs taken. Sophy stared at the photograph, and then she ran to the mirror and stared at her own face. But she had not learned anything from looking at either face, for she sighed and got into bed.

Two or three times she leaned up on her elbow to hear if her mother had gone up to her own room, but she heard no sound, and several times she wanted to go down again and ask to be forgiven, but she knew that instead of coming to terms they would begin to argue again, so she lay still, and began instead to plan the things that she would do for her mother when she had money of her own to spend as she liked. But even this was difficult to do because her mother and herself so rarely liked the same things. The tears came into her eyes.

And then it suddenly seemed to Sophy that she had discovered a secret, a wonderful secret, that wise men had been unable to discover, and yet it was so simple and so clear that anyone could understand it. She would go through the world teaching her message. And when it was understood there would be an end to all the misery and unhappiness, all the misunderstanding and argument with which she had been familiar all her life. Everything would be changed. Everything would be different.

The footsteps that had stopped outside her door moved on, and then were silent. A door closed far away. The dream began to form again. People would all have to become alike. They would have to look alike and speak alike and feel and talk and think alike.

What a wonderful place the world would become. People would all look alike. They would all look like the girls in the photograph, with white dresses and linked arms. They would speak and think alike. They would all think like herself and her father. It was so simple. It was so clear! She was surprised that no one had thought of it before. She saw the girls untwine their arms, and lift up the hems of their long dresses and step aside to admit her as she passed into their company.

Biographical Notes

Mary Lavin was born in America of Irish parents in 1912. When she was 9, the family returned to Ireland and settled in Bective, Co. Meath. At school she was quite studious and read a lot, but had no intention of becoming a writer. Towards the end of her M.A. course in English Literature at University College, Dublin, she tried her hand at writing stories, and was surprised to find that it came easy to her, and that each one was immediately accepted for publication by various literary magazines. Her first collection of stories, Tales from Bective Bridge *(1943), was an immediate success with readers and critics alike.*

Since then she has devoted herself to writing, producing two novels and ten collections of short stories, not including the two-volume Stories of Mary Lavin *(1964 and 1974). Over the years she has been awarded several literary prizes, including the Katherine Mansfield Prize, and two Guggenheim Fellowships. She spent some time in the United States, lecturing and conducting classes in creative writing. Most of her life, however, has been spent in the community she grew up in: for several years now she has owned and run a farm in Bective. Everyday life in such a rural Irish community provides the background for the vast majority of her stories.*

Mary Lavin has three daughters from her first marriage to William Walsh, a lawyer, who died in 1954. In 1969 she married Michael McDonald Scott, Dean of the Dublin School of Irish Studies. She has recently been awarded an honorary D. Litt. by University College, Dublin.

Annotations

49 4 **baleful** sinister, full of ill-will – 13 **hot jars** jars containing hot water for warming a bed – 19 **garrulity** tendency to talk a lot of nonsense – 28 **to mingle** to mix – 29 **cocksfoot, ratstail, clover** plants (weeds) found in a meadow – 32 **offhand** casual, without thinking – **to embolden s.o.** to give s.o. the courage – 33 **hunkers** *coll.* thighs

50 2 **to jerk** to move suddenly – 3 **in dumb show** making gestures, as if one were unable to speak (i.e. dumb) – **study** room for writing and studying in – 4 **fumes** strong-smelling vapours, smoke, etc. – 7 **to scour** [aʊ] to scrub, to clean thoroughly – 12 **flagged** covered with flat stones – 14 **to brood** to think deeply – 16 **degree** academic title acquired by passing an exam – 27 **grudgingly** from **to grudge s.o. s.th.** to be displeased at a person's good luck, happiness, etc. (nicht gönnen) – 36 **bracelet** jewellery worn round one's wrist – 40 **to give a salutation** to greet

51 1 **braid** woven band of silk, etc. used to decorate edges of jackets, etc. – **velvet** soft cloth made mainly of silk (Samt) – 10 **haphazard** without plan or system – 15 **canvas** *here:* oil painting (on canvas) – 20 **to resemble** to be like – 25 **to inherit** [ɪnˈherɪt] to get from one's parents (physical characteristics, temperament, wealth, etc.) – **disposition** character, temperament – 27 **to clasp** to hold tightly – **to scrutinize** to examine closely – 37 **spite** desire to hurt in revenge

52 6 **to urge s.o.** to try to persuade – **10 to pout** [aʊ] to put on an expression of displeasure – 13 **to delude** to deceive – 22 **queer profits** *here: Ir. coll.* a lot of profit – 33 **lassitude** laziness, lack of interest – 34 **disinclination** unwillingness

53 3 **range** coal-burning stove, for heating and cooking – 6 **poultice** ['pəʊltɪs] substance left to dry on the skin to aid healing process – 13 **pantry** room in which food is kept – 14 **dubious** doubtful, uncertain – 16 **grimace** ['grɪməs] twisted facial expression – 27 **concentric** with the same centre – 28 **within the orbit of her olfactory organs** near enough to her nose – 34 **to dilate** to become or make wider – 35 **hair-slide** decorative clip used to hold one's hair in place

54 5 **slippers** light shoes worn indoors – **dressing-gown** light coat worn in bedroom, bathroom, etc. – 7 **boxroom** store-room – 14 **logs** pieces of the branches of a tree – 28 **taken aback** surprised, slightly upset – 34 **irritably** bad-humouredly – 36 **banter** casual, friendly conversation – 39 **paper** *here:* written examination in one part of a subject – 40 **to pull through** *coll.* to pass

55 3 **strain** pressure, stress – 19 **underlinen** underwear – 28 **self-conscious(ly)** feeling uncomfortable and ill at ease – 29 **cuticle** hard skin surrounding one's fingernails – 31 **to crook** to bend – **pincers** tool for pulling things out – 32 **a tug** a pull – 38 **to knit back** to become part of s.th. again

56 11 **to poke up** to stir the coals and make them burn again – 22 **frail** delicate, easily broken – 23 **rim** edge – 26 **incongruous(ly)** seeming to have no connection – 33 **closet** ['klɒzət] cupboard – 34 **to toddle** (of a baby) to walk

57 4 **passion** strong feeling – 15 **tendrils** part of a creeping plant which winds round things – 21 **trying** *adj.* difficult – 23 **abyss** deep, seemingly bottomless hole (Abgrund) – 26 **clasp** (of a bag, box, etc.) part which fastens – 32 **wicker** made of cane, like a basket – 33 **scenic screen** painted landscapes as background for photographs – **trellis balustrades** railing or fence made of criss-cross wooden rods – 34 **posture** position – 36 **to tilt** to bend over – 37 **brooch** [əʊ] decorative pin – 39 **to entwine** to twist, wind around s.th.

58 5 **to entreat** to beg, to ask urgently – 7 **beaux** [bəʊz] young men – **bouquets** [bʊ'keɪz] bunches of flowers – 8 **larks, pranks** escapades, tricks – 19 **asunder** apart – **to rot** to go bad – 25 **a scold** person who is always scolding, complaining criticizing – 33 **scum** *here:* skin on the surface

59 14 **to sip** to drink in very small quantities – 26 **distaste** dislike – 33 **to fling** to throw – 39 **to harp on s.th.** to keep on talking or complaining about s.th. – 40 **out of earshot** too far away to hear

60 1 **to lose one's temper** to become angry – 5 **two (birds) of a feather** two of one kind – 17 **having a slap at** *coll.* criticizing, mocking – 20 **to crow** sound made by a cock – **to cackle** sound made by a chicken or hen – 25 **trait** characteristic – 35 **muslin** light cotton cloth – 40 **stern** hard, serious, determined

61 13 **to come to terms** to agree – 21 **message** information or belief one wants to spread – 34 **hem** lower edge of a dress

Interpretation and Teaching Notes

Background, Content and Analysis

Though not quite as widely acclaimed and anthologized as a number of her other stories, "A Cup of Tea" is one of those which Mary Lavin regards as coming closest to what she wanted to achieve in her writing[1], i.e. to reveal in a flash of insight the truths hidden in the trivial details of her characters' lives. Considering this easily justifiable evaluation, the comparative neglect of this story can perhaps be best explained in terms of widespread expectations as regards the proper subject-matter for an Irish short story.

Probably because of her degree of integration into the mainstream of Irish life, Mary Lavin has never been a self-consciously 'Irish' writer; her interest in social and political themes is in any case less pronounced than that of writers like O'Connor and O'Faolain, whose formative years coincided with the struggle for national independence. To select one of those Lavin stories with a peculiarly 'Irish' theme would therefore give a misleading impression of her work – and of Irish society.

In its concentration on character as opposed to plot, "A Cup of Tea" is clearly differentiated from the rather contrived 'stories with a pattern'[2] with which Mary Lavin experimented in subsequent collections but largely abandoned in her more recent work. Its strength derives to a large extent from a judicious use of shifting point of view. Though the greater part of the third-person narrative is told from the point of view of the daughter who has just arrived home from her final term at university, it is prevented from becoming a simple tale of her exasperation at her mother's demands by switching over at strategic points in the story to the perceptions of the mother. In this way, we are made aware of the equal validity of her feelings and needs, and the inevitability of conflict.

The title of the story refers to its central image. It is one which, in an Irish context, could hardly be exceeded for its connotations of relaxed, informal sociability and person-to-person communication. As the statistics on tea-drinking in Ireland suggest, and as anyone with the slightest acquaintance

1 Cf. Richard F. Peterson, *Mary Lavin*, p. 150; this view was confirmed by Mary Lavin in a letter to the author of these 'Interpretations', 1st March 1981.

2 In the Lavin story entitled "A Story with a Pattern" (*A Single Lady and Other Stories*, London 1951), the protagonist is an author who is criticized for the lack of plot in her stories.

with the country will realize, the first rule of Irish social life is: if in doubt, put on the kettle for a cup of tea.

This is the mother's first instinct as she awaits the arrival of her daughter. In this introductory section of the story, which is told from the point of view of the servant-girl, it soon becomes obvious that it is also a symptom of the mother's exaggerated anxiety to please. The servant's shrewd exploitation of her weaknesses (p. 49, ll. 17–19, 27–28, 32; p. 50, ll. 1–2) is also our first indication that all is not well in the family. One element of potential conflict is obviously her tendency – common to many devoted mothers – to ignore her daughter's real interests. We get the impression (p. 49, ll. 20–23) of a strangely undifferentiated, impersonal kind of love, reduced to the biological tie.

The second deviation from the ideal of a happy family – and, as it turns out, another point of conflict with her daughter – is the mother's badly concealed bitterness towards her husband. This first emerges in her rather strained attempt (p. 50, ll. 16–23) to make a strong distinction between her daughter's and her husband's intellectual achievements. The reasons for the deterioration of her marriage are not made explicit, but there is a strong suggestion that the couple's incompatibility is mirrored in the mother-daughter relationship (cf. p. 59, ll. 39–40). Thus there is considerable tragic irony in the fact that it is in this equally impossible relationship that the mother seeks compensation for the failure of her marriage.

All of these mutually destructive tendencies come out in the way the mother greets her daughter: any thought of Sophy's likeness to her father is immediately suppressed, or even expressly denied (p. 50, l. 37 – p. 51, l. 3; p. 51, ll. 16–25); the shower of questions (ll. 4–14) betrays a love for her daughter (as a daughter) which is combined with a total lack of interest in her as a person. At the point where the mother realizes (p. 51, ll. 26–31) that, far from winning over her daughter to her side, her adverse comments about her husband are only alienating Sophy from her, there is a switch to the daughter's viewpoint: we see that both mother and daughter are now on guard, careful to avoid open conflict.

From here on the mother's tactic is to feign concern for her husband, who seems to be a bit of a recluse, immersed in his hobby, and never leaving his study unless he absolutely has to. Her show of urging Sophy to go up to him "if only for a minute" comes across, however, as a tragicomic charade (p. 51, l. 35 – p. 52, l. 28). Though the mother's bitterness is never far from the surface (p. 51, ll. 36–38; p. 52, ll. 18–25), Sophy plays along out of pity.

During Sophy's hour-long absence upstairs, her mother's actions betray her agitated state of mind: she fusses over this and that, snaps at the maid, and unnecessarily boils the milk for the tea, just to "make sure of it". When Sophy finally does emerge from her father's study, the mother's efforts seem for a while to have paid off: the late-night cup of tea starts off on a promising note (p. 54, ll. 9–21). Their conversation soon deteriorates, however, into predictable patterns. The passage on page 55, lines 1–15 is particularly revealing: the mother's well-meaning concern about the "strain" university puts "on a girl" cannot but be mildly insulting to Sophy, who obviously takes her studies seriously. When Sophy – ignoring the jibe at her father – tries to correct such mistaken ideas, all her mother registers is her "glossy silk knees and nice straight hair" before coming out with another stream of excited, unrelated questions.

The next section of the story is devoted mainly to the desire for harmony on both sides. The mother's ideal of harmony is presented in the form of her childhood memories: her intimacy with her own mother, their chats about dances, clothes, needlework, hair-styles, etc. For Sophy, a harmony of sorts can only be assured through the avoidance of open conflict; when her mother's confidences threaten – as is often the case – to lead onto dangerous ground, she rapidly changes the subject (e.g. p. 56, l. 20). This, predictably, infuriates her mother, whose self-control is at this point seen to be largely a function of her ideas of middle-class propriety: she would have thrown the cup on the floor "only it was belonging to a set" (p. 57, ll. 4–5).

The pity Sophy feels for her mother (ll. 12 ff.) springs from her realization that her somewhat ridiculous and contradictory statements (ll. 7–11) – and even her continual griping about her husband – are but the surface manifestations of her very real loneliness and isolation. The old photograph to which Sophy turns in another attempt to change the subject makes it easy for her (and for the reader) to imagine what it must be like for her mother: brought up in a cosy world of "beaux and bouquets" (p. 58, l. 7), conditioned to seek her sole fulfilment in marriage and motherhood, she must now feel cheated by reality. This realization gives rise in Sophy to a number of conflicting thoughts and emotions (ll. 9–19): in linking her mother's youthful illusions with her own present situation, she is torn between confidence that people are more realistic nowadays, and fear that this may not be so. In any case, she is now tired, irritated and a lot less sure of her own position.

The tangle of suppressed emotions on both sides could be likened at this point to an explosive mixture just waiting for a spark: it comes in the form of a ridiculous disagreement about whether boiled milk spoils the taste of tea. Significantly, this pretext has been unwittingly supplied by the mother in her anxiety to please, a fact she now realizes (p. 59, ll. 25–31). Her sense of the unfairness of it all causes her to hit back in a way that allows some aspects of their real conflict to emerge. Even when Sophy gets back to the subject of boiled milk in tea, the undercurrents are unmistakable (p. 60, ll. 9–19), and a head-on clash on the subject of the father can no longer be avoided. It ends with an angry slamming of doors.

In her bedroom, where the floor "had been waxed twice over", Sophy regrets her outburst and is reminded of her earlier insight that her mother cannot have foreseen the trap her marriage would turn into, any more than she herself can be sure the young man in the photograph she carries around with her is really suited to her (p. 60, l. 34 – p. 61, l. 9). But she knows that any attempt to apologize would probably make matters worse. Their differences in outlook even make it difficult for her to imagine a reconciliation in the future.

In this frame of mind, she falls asleep, and her dream testifies to the attraction the idyllic tableau of harmony in the old photograph held for her. Freed from the bonds of logic and reality, she grasps at a beautifully simple solution which links the harmony her mother craves with her own personality and intellect. It is patently absurd, but – one realizes – no more so than the contradictory though nonetheless real human needs and longings that have emerged in the course of the evening.

First Unit
The Characters and Their Relationships

Preparation: Though this story should, ideally, be read in one piece, for the first unit it is only necessary for the students to have read to p. 54, l. 8.

1. The characters and the basic situation

List the characters who appear in the story, and discuss their relative importance.

In order of 'appearance': the maid – a minor character, whose remarks help to introduce the theme of the story; the mother and Sophy, both central characters; Sophy's father, who does not strictly speaking 'appear' in the story, but whose presence is felt by the other two members of the family, and who affects their relationship with one another.

What is the situation at the beginning of the story?

A mother is expecting her daughter home for the holidays after her exams at the university.

2. The mother

What does the mother reveal about

- *herself?*
- *her attitude to her daughter?*
- *her attitude to her husband?*

Right at the beginning of the story she is portrayed as a house-proud, middleclass housewife, with a maid to help her. Her fussing over the arrival of her daughter reflects intense maternal love (p. 51, ll. 8–11), which is not, however, accompanied by any real interest in her daughter as a person in her own right (p. 49, ll. 20–23; p. 51, ll. 12–16); the questions she asks about her examination seem to be purely attempts to win her daughter's trust.
Recognition of Sophy's achievements (p. 50, ll. 16–23) is linked with disparaging remarks about her husband and his hobby – and remarks about her appearance (p. 51, ll. 16–25) with efforts to minimize her daughter's likeness to her husband. Whatever affection once existed between herself and her husband has long since died (p. 50, l. 35 – p. 51, l. 2), and only bitterness remains in its place: she seems to be deeply hurt by his rejection of her company (p. 52, ll. 18–26).

3. The daughter

Now do the same for Sophy.

An intelligent young woman, student of economics and political science, just finished final exams; has a good relationship with her father, with whom she has plenty to talk about (p. 52, ll. 31–36; p. 54, ll. 5–7). She attempts to play this down (p. 52, ll. 10–13) out of a sense of duty to her mother – she wants to be kind to her, but can find no common ground – her mother's caustic remarks about her father set up a barrier, and she probably senses her mother's lack of genuine interest.

4. The conflict
Sum up the 'triangle' of feelings in a diagram, and point out where the tension seems to be greatest.

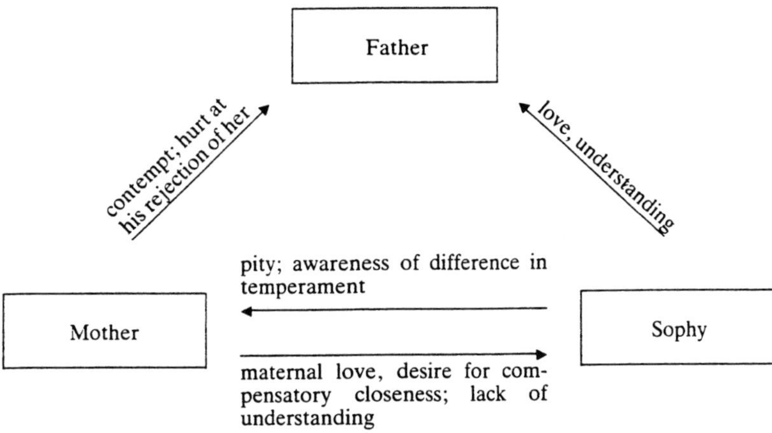

The mother's efforts to win her daughter's love and trust are so bound up with her contempt for Sophy's father, and with a disregard for Sophy's real feelings and interests, that they are bound to have the opposite effect.

Homework: Re-read the story (or read to end) and pick out all the references to tea, tea-cups, milk, the kettle, etc.

Second Unit
The Storm in a Tea-Cup

1. The significance of the various references to 'tea'
In what connection is the 'cup of tea' referred to – before the quarrel breaks out? What function is served by such references in the story?

P. 49, ll. 1–3: mother's anxious anticipation of her daughter's arrival.
P. 53, ll. 10–12: further example of the mother's 'fussing'.
P. 53, l. 13 – p. 54, l. 3: the suspicion that the milk may be on the verge of going sour causes the mother to boil it, to be absolutely sure it will be all right for Sophy's tea – she thus unwittingly provides the pretext for a quarrel; in addition, her behaviour towards the maid betrays a certain irritability and lack of self-confidence.
P. 54, ll. 13–21: the mother's hopes show signs of being fulfilled – drinking tea together as an opportunity for a long, friendly chat.
P. 56, l. 20 – p. 57, l. 5: for Sophy, the hand-painted cups offer an opportunity to change the subject and prevent her mother from complaining about her father; for her mother, this is a deliberate frustration of her desire to confide in her daughter.
P. 57, ll. 6–10: this stresses the mother's loneliness and isolation.
P. 57, ll. 19–21: the mother's desire to make her daughter understand how she feels becomes particularly evident; a conflict seems unavoidable.
P. 58, ll. 20–27: a reminder of the mother's irritating tendency to overdo the 'mothering'.
In short, all the elements of potential conflict are linked with this image, or set of images.

2. The old photograph
What does the old photograph mean to Sophy in the context of the story – and how does it affect her attitude to her mother?
The photo album is first of all (p. 57, ll. 22–26) another opportunity to direct the conversation to less dangerous ground. The picture she opens it at happens to be one which has always fascinated her. It suggests a number of contrasts:

an idyllic, idealized past --	a complicated present
family harmony ------	conflict
her mother's dreams ----	her mother's unhappiness and isolation
her own dreams ------	?

As well as deepening her awareness of the shortcomings of the present situation, it makes Sophy less sure of her own position and less capable of openly criticizing her mother.

3. The quarrel
Describe the quarrel which ensues. What is it really about?
On the surface, a trivial squabble about whether milk for the tea should be

boiled or not; on another level, it is an outlet for frustrated emotions on both sides.
Sophy: irritation at her mother's exaggerated demands on her, which she is temperamentally unable to fulfil; loyalty to her father.
Mother: frustration and disappointment that she has failed to win her daughter's love and approval, which she so badly needs as a compensation for the shortcomings of her marriage; the realization (p. 59, ll. 25–31) that it is her own anxiety to please that has supplied the pretext for Sophy's outburst.
From p. 59, l. 39 on, it becomes clear that the quarrel has arisen from their irreconcilable differences and conflicting needs, as exemplified by Sophy's closeness to, and her mother's estrangement from the (unseen) father.

4. Sophy's dream
What is Sophy's state of mind after the quarrel with her mother? Why doesn't she apologize?
She feels guilty and would like to apologize, but realizes that she is temperamentally incapable of preventing another quarrel from developing; she tries, and fails, to imagine a solution in the future.
What is the meaning of Sophy's dream?
She dreams of a world in which all people are alike – like herself and her father. Her conscious self has had to admit that there is no satisfactory solution, that people – including herself – cannot help being different; when freed from the bonds of logic her desire for harmony and peace makes her reach out for a simple solution.

Homework: (written comment) To what extent would the conflict between Sophy and her mother be different if it were to take place today?

Third Unit
Patterns of Conflict in Family Life

Note: This unit should take the form of an open discussion in which the students are free to relate the story to their own experience of family life and interpersonal relations in general.

Suggested procedure:
a) List the various reasons for the conflict in Sophy's family.

b) State them in general terms as far as possible.
c) Relate them to the students' own experience of family life.

1. *The estrangement of Sophy's parents*: Here one could discuss Sophy's statement (p. 58, ll. 18–19) that "marriages may break asunder nowadays, but they don't rot slowly".

2. *Sophy and her mother differ in temperament, outlook, tastes, interests.* This can be generalized in the form of the simple truth that people differ, even within families.

3. *The mother doesn't want to accept that Sophy is different.* In general terms: parents tend to expect their children to be similar to themselves, to share their values, etc., and often have difficulty in respecting their 'separateness'. One could discuss whether there is a greater tolerance of such differences today, or whether such conflict is a part of human nature (cf. the students' own relationships with their parents: will they be more tolerant of differences in their own children?).

4. *The mother was brought up in a period very different from the world of her daughter* (presumably turn of the century, Victorian or Edwardian era, as opposed to the 1930s–40s). In general terms: the 'generation gap'. Points to discuss: Is there always such a difference between the society parents grew up in and that of their children? Must this lead to misunderstandings and conflict? What problems arise when parents whose formative years were in (say) the fifties cannot come to terms with the world of the eighties?

5. *The mother expected to find her sole fulfilment and happiness in marriage and motherhood.* Consequences for herself: disillusionment, emptiness, she has nothing to give meaning to her life. Consequences for her husband: her narrow view of life is presumably an element in their incompatibility. Consequences for her daughter: impossible demands, conflict with Sophy's more 'modern' outlook. Note that Sophy was one of a minority at the time (cf. p. 50, ll. 17–20). It should be discussed to what extent things are different today, whether the relative 'backwardness' of the post-war years in the field of women's rights affects the attitudes of the students' parents, and whether sex-role stereotyping is a point of conflict in their own homes.

For Further Study

Points for discussion

1. Study the narrative technique of 'selective omniscience' as used in this story.
2. Characterize the father, on the basis of the evidence given by his wife and his daughter.

Courses/Projects based on this story

1. Stories by Mary Lavin
"A Cup of Tea" plus a selection of the following:
- "Sarah"
- "At Sallygap"
- "The Green Grave and the Black Grave"
- "Miss Holland"

} from *Tales from Bective Bridge*, Poolbeg paperback, Dublin 1978

- "The Story of the Widow's Son" – included in *British Short Stories of Today* (Hirschgraben) and *Seven Anglo-American Short Stories* (Diesterweg)
- "The Patriot Son" – simplified version in *One True Friend and Other Irish Short Stories* (Longman-Langenscheidt)
- "The Will" – included in *Irish Short Stories* (Schöningh)

2. The Family
- "A Cup of Tea"
- Frank O'Connor, "My Oedipus Complex" (see p. 48)
- The chapter "Personal Relations" in *Life, Language, Literature* (Klett)

Michael McLaverty

Father Christmas

"Will you do what I ask you?" his wife said again, wiping the crumbs off the newspaper which served as a tablecloth. "Wear your hard hat and you'll get the job."

He didn't answer her or raise his head. He was seated on the dilapidated sofa lacing his boots, and behind him tumbled two of his children, each chewing a crust of bread. His wife paused, a hand on her hip. She glanced at the sleety rain falling into the backyard, turned round, and threw the crumbs into the fire.

"You'll wear it, John – won't you?"

Again he didn't answer though his mind was already made up. He strode into the scullery and while he washed himself she took an overcoat from a nail behind the kitchen door, brushed it vigorously, gouging out the specks of dirt with the nose of the brush. She put it over the back of a chair and went upstairs for his hard hat.

"I'm a holy show in that article," he said, when she was handing him the hat and helping him into the overcoat. "I'll be a nice ornament among the other applicants! I wish you'd leave me alone!"

"You look respectable anyhow. I could take a fancy for you all over again," and she kissed him playfully on the side of the cheek.

"If I don't get the job you needn't blame me. I've done all you asked – every mortal thing."

"You'll get it all right – never you fear. I know what I'm talking about."

He hurried out of the street in case some of the neighbours would ask him if he were going to a funeral, and when he had taken his place in the line of young men who were all applying for the job of Father Christmas in the Big Store he was still conscious of the bowler hat perched on top of his head. He was a timid little man and he tried to crouch closer to the wall and make himself inconspicuous amongst that group of grey-capped men. The rain continued to fall as they waited for the door to open and he watched the drops clinging to the peaks of their caps, swelling and falling to the ground.

"If he had a beard we could all go home," he heard someone say, and he felt his ears reddening, aware that the remark was cast at him. But later when he was following the Manager up the brass-lipped stairs, after he had got the job, he dwelt on the wisdom of his wife and knew that the hat had endowed him with an air of shabby respectability.

"Are you married?" the Manager had asked him, looking at the nervous way he turned the hat in his hand. "And have you any children?" He had answered everything with a meek smile and the Manager told him to stand aside until he had interviewed, as a matter of form, the rest of the applicants.

And then the interviews were quickly over, and when the Manager and John were mounting the stairs he saw a piece of caramel paper sticking to the Manager's heel. Down a long aisle they passed with rows of counters at each side and shoppers gathered round them. And though it was daylight outside, the electric lights were lit, and through the glare there arose a buzz of talk, the rattle of money, and the warm smell of new clothes and perfume and confectionery – all of it entering John's mind in a confused and dreamy fashion, for his eye was fastened on the caramel paper as he followed respectfully after the Manager. Presently they emerged on a short flight of stairs where a notice – PRIVATE – on trestles straddled across it. The Manager lifted it ostentatiously to the side, ushered John forward with a sweep of his arm, and replaced the notice with mechanical importance.

"Just a minute," said John, and he plucked the caramel paper from the Manager's heel, crumpled it between his fingers, and put it in his pocket.

They entered the quiet seclusion of a small room that had a choking smell of dust and cardboard boxes. The Manager mounted a step-ladder, and taking a large box from the top shelf looked at something written on the side, slapped the dust off it against his knee, and broke the string.

"Here," he said, throwing down the box. "You'll get a red cloak in that and a white beard." He sat on the top rung of the ladder and held a false face on the tip of his finger: "Somehow I don't think you'll need this. You'll do as you are. Just put on the beard and whiskers."

"Whatever you say," smiled John, for he always tried to please people.

Another box fell at his feet: "You'll get a pair of top boots in that!" The Manager folded the step-ladder, and daintily picking pieces of fluff from his sleeves he outlined John's duties for the day and emphasised that after closing-time he'd have to make up parcels for the following day's sale.

Left alone John breathed freely, took off his overcoat and hung it at the back of the door, and for some reason whenever he crossed the floor he did so on his tiptoes. He lifted the red cloak that was trimmed with fur, held it in his outstretched arms to admire it, and squeezed the life out of a moth that was struggling in one of the folds. Chips of tinsel glinted on the shoulders of the cloak and he was ready to flick them off when he decided it was more

Christmassy-looking to let them remain on. He pulled on the cloak, crossed on tiptoes to a looking-glass on the wall and winked and grimaced at himself, sometimes putting up the collar of the cloak to enjoy the warm touch of the fur on the back of his neck. He attached the beard and the whiskers, spitting out one or two hairs that had strayed into his mouth.

"The very I-T," he said, and caught the beard in his fist and waggled it at his reflection in the mirror. "Hello, Santa!" he smiled, and thought of his children and how they would laugh to see him togged up in this regalia. "I must tell her to bring them down some day," and he gave a twirl on his toes, making a heap of paper rustle in the corner.

He took off his boots, looked reflectively at the broken sole of each and pressed his thumb into the wet leather. "Pasteboard – nothing else!" he said in disgust, and threw them on the heap of brown paper. He reached for the top boots that were trimmed with fur. They looked a bit on the small side. With some difficulty he squeezed his feet into them. He walked across the floor, examining the boots at each step; they were very tight for him, but he wasn't one to complain, and, after all, the job was only for the Christmas season and they'd be sure to stretch with the wearing.

When he was fully dressed he made his way down the stairs, lifted his leg over the trestle with the word PRIVATE and presented himself on one of the busy floors. A shopgirl, hesitating before striking the cash-register, smiled over at him. His face burned. Then a little girl plucked her mother's skirt and called, "Oh, Mammy, there's Daddy Christmas!" With his hands in his wide sleeves he stood in a state of nervous perplexity till the shop-girl, scratching her head with the tip of her pencil, shouted jauntily: "First Floor, Santa Claus, right on down the stairs!" He stumbled on the stairs because of the tight boots and when he halted to regain his composure he felt the blood hammering in his temples and he wished now that he hadn't listened to his wife and worn his hard hat. She was always nagging at him, night, noon and morning, and he doing his damned best!

On the first floor the Manager beckoned him to a miniature house – a house painted in imitation brick, snow on the eaves, a door which he could enter by stooping low, and a chimney large enough to contain his head and shoulders, and inside the house stacks of boxes neatly piled, some in blue paper and others in pink.

The Manager produced a hand-bell. "You stand here," said the Manager, placing himself at the door of the house. "Ring your bell a few times – like this. Then shout in a loud, commanding voice: 'Roll up now! Blue for the Boys, and Pink for the Girls'." And he explained that when business was slack, he was to mount the ladder, descend the chimney, and bring up the parcels in that manner, but if there was a crowd he was just to open the door and shake hands with each child before presenting the boxes. They were all the same price – a shilling each.

For the first ten minutes or so John's voice was weak and self-conscious and the Manager, standing a short distance away, ordered him to raise his voice a little louder: "You must attract attention – that's what you're paid for. Try it once again."

"Blue for the Boys, and Pink for the Girls!" shouted John, and he imagined all the buyers at the neighbouring counters had paused to listen to him. "Blue for the Boys, and Pink for the Girls!" he repeated, his eye on the Manager who was judging him from a distance. The Manager smiled his approval and then shook an imaginary bell in the air. John suddenly remembered about the bell in his hand and he shook it vigorously, but a shop-girl tightened up her face at him and he folded his fingers over the skirt of the bell in order to muffle the sound. He gained more confidence, but as his nervousness decreased he became aware of the tight boots imprisoning his feet, and occasionally he would disappear into his little house and catching the sole of each in turn he would stretch them across his knee.

But the children gave him no peace, and with his head held genially to the side, if the Manager were watching him, he would smile broadly and listen with affected interest to each child's demand.

"Please, Santa Claus, bring me a tricycle at Christmas and a doll's pram for Angela."

"I'll do that! Everything you want," said Father Christmas expansively, and he patted the little boy on the head with gentle dignity before handing him a blue parcel. But when he raised his eyes to the boy's mother she froze him with a look.

"I didn't think you would have any tricycles this year," she said. "I thought you were only making wooden trains."

"Oh, yes! No, yes. Not at all! Yes, of course, I'll get you a nice wooden train," Father Christmas turned to the boy in his confusion. "If you keep good I'll have a lovely train for you."

"I don't want an oul train. I want a tricycle," the boy whimpered, clutching his blue-papered parcel.

"I couldn't make any tricycles this year," consoled Father Christmas. "My reindeers was sick and three of them died on me."

The boy's mother smiled and took him by the hand. "Now, pet, didn't I tell you Santa had no tricycles? You better shout up the chimney for something else – a nice game or a wooden train."

"I don't want an oul game, I want a tricycle," he cried, and jigged his feet.

"You'll get a warm ear if you're not careful. Come on now and none of your nonsense. And Daddy Christmas after giving you a nice box, all for yourself."

Forcibly she led the boy away and John, standing with his hands in his sleeves, felt the prickles of sweat on his forehead and resolved to promise nothing to the children until he had got the cue from the parents.

As the day progressed he climbed up the ladder and down the chimney, emerging again with his arms laden with parcels. His feet tortured him and when he glanced at the boots every wrinkle in the leather was smoothed away. He couldn't continue like this all day; it would drive him mad.

"Roll up!" he bawled. "Roll up! Blue for the Pinks and Boys for the Girls! Roll up, I say. Blue for the Pinks and Boys for the Girls." Then he stopped and repeated the same mistake before catching himself up. And once more he clanged the bell with subdued ferocity till its sound drowned the jingle of the cash-registers and the shop-girls had to shout to be heard.

At one o'clock he wearily climbed the stairs to the quiet room, where dinner was brought to him on a tray. He took off his boots and gazed sympathetically at his crushed toes. He massaged them tenderly, and when he had finished his dinner he pared his corns with a razor blade he had bought at one of the counters. He now squeezed his bare feet into the boots, walked across the room, and sat down again, his face twisted with despair. "Why do I always give in to that woman," he said aloud to himself. "I've no strength – no power to stand up and shout in her face: 'No, no, no! I'll go my own way in my own time!'" He'd let her know tonight the agony he suffered, and his poor feet gathered up all day like a rheumatic fist.

Calmed after this outburst, and reassuring himself that the job was only for three weeks, he gave a whistle of forced satisfaction, brushed the corn-parings off the chair, and went off to stand outside the little house with its imitation snow on the chimney.

The afternoon was the busiest time, and he was glad to be able to stand at the door like a human being and hand out the parcels, instead of ascending and descending the ladder like a trained monkey. When the children crowded too close to him he kept them at arm's length in case they'd trample on his feet. But he always managed to smile as he watched them shaking their boxes or tearing holes in the paper in an effort to guess what was inside. And the parents smiled too when they looked at him wagging his finger at the little girls and promising them dolls at Christmas if they would go to bed early, eat their porridge and stop biting their nails. But before closing time a woman was back holding an untidy parcel. "That's supposed to be for a boy," she said peevishly.

"There's a rubber doll in it and my wee boy has cried his eyes out ever since."

"I'm just new to the job," Father Christmas apologised. "It'll never occur again." And he tossed the parcel into the house and handed the woman a new one.

At the end of his day he had gathered from the floor a glove with a hole in one finger, three handkerchiefs, a necklace of blue beads, and a child's handbag containing a halfpenny and three tram-tickets. When he was handing them to the Manager he wondered if he should complain about the boots, but the tired look on the Manager's face and his reminder about staying behind to make up parcels discouraged him.

For the last time he climbed the stairs, took off his boots and flung them from him, and as he prepared the boxes he padded about the cool floor in his bare feet, and to ensure that he wouldn't make a mistake he arranged, at one side of the room, the contents for the girls' boxes: dolls, shops, pages of transfers, story books, and crayons; and at the opposite side of the room the toys for the boys: ludo, snakes and ladders, blow football, soldiers, cowboy outfits, and wooden whistles. And as he parcelled them neatly and made loops in the twine for the children's fingers he decided once again to tell his wife to bring his own kids along and he'd have special parcels prepared for them.

On his way out of the Store the floors were silent and deserted, the counters humped with canvas covers, and the little house looking strangely real now under a solitary light. A mouse nibbling at something on the floor scurried off between an alleyway in the counters, and on the ground floor two women were sweeping up the dust and gossiping loudly.

The caretaker let him out by a side door, and as he walked off in the rain through the lamp-lighted streets he put up the collar of his coat and avoided the puddles as best he could. A sullen resentment seized his heart and he began to drag from the corners of his mind the things that irritated him. He thought they should have given him his tea before he left, or even a bun and a glass of milk, and he thought of his home and maybe the fine tea his wife would have for him, and a good fire in the grate and the kids in bed. He walked more quickly. He passed boys eating chip potatoes out of a newspaper, and he stole a glance at Joe Raffo's chip-shop and the cloud of steam rolling through the open door into the cold air. The smell maddened him. He plunged his hands into his pockets and fiddled with a button, bits of hard crumbs, and a sticky bit of caramel paper. He took out the caramel paper and threw it on the wet street.

He felt cheated and discontented with everything; and the more he thought of the job the more he blamed his wife for all the agony he had suffered throughout the day. She couldn't leave him alone – not for one solitary minute could she let him have a thought of his own or come to a decision of his own. She must be for ever interfering, barging in, and poking into his business. He was a damned fool to listen to her and to don a ridiculous hard hat for such a miserable job. Father Christmas and his everlasting smile! He'd smile less if he had to wear a pair of boots three sizes too small for him. It was a young fella they wanted for the job – somebody accustomed to standing for hours at a street corner and measuring the length of his spits on the kerb. And then the ladder! That was the bloody limit! Up and down, down and up, like a squirrel in a cage, instead of giving you a stick and a chair where you could sit and really look like an old man. When he'd get home he'd let his wife know what she let him in for. It would lead to a row between them, and when that happened she'd go about for days flinging his meals on the table and belting the kids for sweet damn-all. He'd have to tell her – it was no use suffering devil's torture and saying nothing about it. But then, it's more likely than not she'd put on her hat and coat and go down to the Manager in the morning and complain about the boots, and then he might lose the job, bad and all as it was. Och, he'd say nothing – sure, bad temper never got you anywhere!

He stepped into a puddle to avoid a man's umbrella and when he felt the cold splash of water up the leg of his trousers his anger surged back again. He'd tell her all. He'd soon take the wind out of her sails and her self-praise about the hat! He'd tell her everything.

He hurried up the street and at the door of his house he let down the collar of his coat and shook the rain off his hat. He listened for a minute and heard the children shouting. He knocked, and the three of them pounded to the door to open it.

"It's Daddy," they shouted, but he brushed past them without speaking.

His wife was washing the floor in the kitchen and as she wrung the cloth into the bucket and brushed back her hair with the back of her hand she looked at him with a bright smile.

"You got it all right?"

"Why aren't the children in bed?"

"I didn't expect you home so soon."

"Did you think I was a bus conductor!"

She noticed the hard ring in his voice. She rubbed the soap on the scrubber and hurried to finish her work, making great whorls and sweeps with the cloth. She took off her dirty apron, and as she washed and dried her hands in the scullery she glanced in at him seated on the sofa, his head resting on his hands, the three children waiting for him to speak to them. "It was the hat," she said to herself. "It was the hat did the trick."

"Come on now and up to bed quickly," and she clapped her hands at the children.

"But you have to wash our legs in the bucket."

"You'll do all right for tonight. Your poor father's hungry after his hard day's work." And as she pulled off a jersey she held it in her hand and gave the fire a poke under the kettle. John stared into the fire and when he raised his foot there was a damp imprint left on the tiles. She handed him a pair of warm socks from the line and a pair of old slippers that she had made for him out of pasteboard and a piece of velours.

"I've a nice bit of steak for your tea," she said. "I'll put on the pan when I get these ones into their beds."

He rubbed his feet and pulled on the warm socks. It was good that she hadn't the steak fried and lying as dry as a stick in the oven. When all was said and done, she had some sense in her head.

The children began to shout up the chimney telling Santa Claus what they wanted for Christmas, and when they knelt to say their prayers they had to thank God for sending their Daddy a good job. John smiled for the first time since he came into the house and he took the youngest on his knee. "You'll get a doll and a pram for Christmas," he said, "and Johnny will get a wooden train with real wheels and Pat – what will we get him?" And he remembered putting a cowboy's outfit into one of the boxes. "A cowboy's outfit – hat and gun."

His wife had put the pan on the fire and already the steak was frizzling. "Don't let that pan burn till I come down again. I'll not be a minute."

He heard her put the kids to bed, and in a few minutes she was down again, a fresh blouse on her and a clean apron.

She poured out his tea and after he had taken a few mouthfuls he began to tell her about the crowd of applicants and about the fellow who shouted: "We'd better all go home," when he had seen him in the hat.

"He was jealous – that's what was wrong with him!" she said. "A good clout on the ear he needed."

He told her about the Manager, the handbell, the blue and pink parcels, the little house, and the red cloak he had to wear. Then he paused, took a drink of tea, cut a piece of bread into three bits, and went on eating slowly.

"It's well you took my advice and wore the hat," she said brightly. "I knew what I was talking about. And you look so – so manly in it." She remembered about the damp stain on the floor, and she lifted his boots off the fender and looked at the broken soles. "They're done," she said, "that's the first call on your wages at the end of the week."

He got up from the table and sat near the fire. She handed him his pipe filled with tobacco, and as she washed the dishes in the scullery she would listen to the little pouts he made while he smoked. Now and again she glanced in at him, at the contented look on his face and the steam arising from his boots on the fender.

She took off her apron, tidied her hair at the looking-glass, and powdered her face. She stole across the floor to him as he sat staring into the fire. Quietly she took the pipe from his lips and put it on the mantelpiece. She smiled at him and he smiled back, and as she stooped to kiss him he knew that he would say nothing to her now about the tight boots.

Biographical Notes

Michael McLaverty is closely associated with the troubled province of Ulster. He was born in 1907 in Monaghan (a county which was to become part of the Irish Republic) and educated mainly in Belfast. After graduating from Queen's University, Belfast, he worked as a teacher, and eventually became headmaster of a secondary school. He remained a dedicated teacher all his life, and though he is now retired, he still continues to do a little teaching in his school in a working-class area of Belfast.

His first novel, Call My Brother Back, *was published in 1939. Like a number of his later novels and stories, it centres on the political unrest which has characterized life in Northern Ireland for so long. When re-issued in 1970 its political relevance made it a best-seller, and revived interest in his short stories, which had been somewhat neglected up to then. He is now generally regarded as one of the most accomplished of Irish writers of fiction.*

Though best known for his treatment of the 'troubles', Michael McLaverty is less concerned with the political issues as such, than with the human aspects of life against a background of violence and bigotry. Most of his short stories deal with the less dramatic aspects of life in the North of Ireland – the everyday concerns of its farmers and fishermen, its teachers, nuns, housewives and schoolchildren. The story we have included in our collection is a representative example of his work in this respect, and in addition, highlights one of the social problems which underlies much of the unrest in Ulster.

Annotations

64 4 **dilapidated** [–'– – – –] very old, worn and shabby – 7 **sleety** mixed with snow – 11 **scullery** small room for washing, adjoining a kitchen in which meals are taken – 12 **to gouge** [gaʊdʒ] to scrape out – 15 **a holy show** *Ir. coll.* a ridiculous sight – 21 **every mortal thing** *Ir. coll.* absolutely everything – 27 **to crouch** [aʊ] to bend, to lower one's height – 28 **inconspicuous** not easily noticed – 33 **brass-lipped** with brass (Messing) at the edges

65 1 **to dwell on** to think about for some time – 5 **meek** humble – 9 **caramel** a kind of sweet – 10 **aisle** [aɪl] passage – 17 **trestle** support consisting of two pairs of wooden legs – **to straddle** to stand with the legs on both sides of s.th. – 18 **ostentatious** showy, demonstrative – **to usher** [ʌ] to show s.o. the way – 29 **whiskers** hair at both sides of a man's face – 32 **daintily** with very fine movements – 39 **tinsel** shiny substance used to decorate Christmas trees, etc.

66 2 **to grimace** ['grɪməs] to twist up one's face with displeasure – 6 **the very I-T** *dated sl.* the real thing – 8 **togged** dressed – 12 **pasteboard** stiff material made from paper – 25 **jauntily** [ɔ:] in a lively way – 27 **composure** [–'– –] self-control, calmness – 30 **and he doing ...** *Ir. coll.* (transl. from Gaelic) even though he was doing ... – 32 **eaves** part of roof which hangs out over a wall – 33 **to stoop** to bend down – 39 **business is slack** there are few customers

67 4 **self-conscious** shy – 13 **vigorously** energetically – 15 **to muffle** to deaden (a sound) – 19 **genially** in a friendly, fatherly way – 33 **oul** [aʊl] *Ir. dial.* old (expressing contempt) – 36 **died on me** *Ir. coll.* sind mir weggestorben – 40 **to jig** to move as if dancing a jig

68 2 **And (he) after giving you** *Ir.* (transl. from Gaelic) now that he has given you – 6 **cue** hint, indication of what one should say – 11 **roll up** traditional fairground cry – **to bawl** to shout – 14 **to subdue** to quieten down – **ferocity** [–'– – –] wildness, aggressiveness – 19 **to pare corns** to cut a layer of hardened skin off one's toes – 40 **peevishly** bad-humouredly

69 1 **wee** *N.Ir.* and *Scot. dial.* little – 16 **transfers** pictures and motifs that can be transferred to various surfaces – 17 **ludo** game played on a board ('Mensch Ärgere Dich Nicht') – **snakes and ladders** game like 'ludo' – 19 **twine** string – 31 **bun** small cake

70 4 **to barge in** to come in without caring whether one is welcome or not – 5 **to don** to put on – 8 **fella** *sl.* fellow – 10 **kerb** edge of footpath – 15 **to belt** to hit hard – **sweet damn-all** *sl.* nothing – 19 **Och** [ɒx] *N.Ir.* and *Scot.* exclamation – 20 **sure** [ʃər] *Ir.* conjunction indicating mild opposition – 22 **to surge** [ɜ:] **back** to come back, like a wave

71 8 **to give the fire a poke** *coll.* to stir up the coals – 12 **tea** *here: Ir.* supper – 33 **clout** [aʊ] slap, box in the ear

72 5 **pouts** [aʊ] *here:* puffs of smoke

Interpretation and Teaching Notes

Background, Content and Analysis

The associations aroused by the title "Father Christmas" inevitably colour the reader's reactions to the story itself. To an extent, our expectations are fulfilled: the action of the story takes place at Christmas-time, the central character is a man playing the role of Santa Claus, and there is humour and sentiment a-plenty. But the scenes of seasonal jollity, the tinsel and the pink and blue parcels, are juxtaposed against scenes of a most un-Christmas-like greyness: sleety rain in the streets of Belfast, worn-out shoes, and lines of grey-capped unemployed men.

The social background of the story is provided by the unemployment which has been endemic in Northern Ireland since the 1920s. At the worst of times, the decline of the shipbuilding industry put over 30 per cent of Belfast's working population on the dole.[1] In the story, the queue of men eager to get such a badly-paid, temporary job as that of Santa Claus in a big store (p. 64, ll. 23–32) hints at such a recession. In the particular situation of Northern Ireland, the competition for the few jobs available, combined with religious discrimination on the part of employers, often led to outbreaks of sectarian violence. But there is no trace of political tensions in this story. Though most of McLaverty's stories have to do with the Catholic community of Northern Ireland, there is no way of telling, from the story itself, whether John and his wife are Catholics or Protestants – it is irrelevant to the point of the story.

If the 'Christmassy' elements function as a foil to the dreary social reality, the social criticism implied by the juxtaposition of these two contrasting aspects remains subordinate to the depiction of the psychological reality of John's situation. This is achieved by means of a double narrative perspective: whereas the greater part of the third-person narrative views John and the other characters from the outside, as it were, the author/narrator not only concentrates on what John sees and hears, but frequently presents his thoughts and feelings directly, in the form of substitutionary narration (e.g. p. 66, ll. 16–18). In this way, the reader is given the opportunity to sympathize with John, while at the same time being aware of his weaknesses.

The first few lines of the story not only establish the setting (a slum

1 Cf. Liam de Paor, *Divided Ulster*, pp. 102–106

dwelling) and the situation (application for a job), but also touch on John's central weakness – his inability to stand up for himself. We see him accepting his wife's benevolent tyranny for the simple reason that she does seem to know best (cf. p. 65, ll. 1–2), while at the same time making a token effort to establish his separate identity by means of his ineffectual grumbling. The lack of self-confidence hinted at in this domestic scene is depicted in a more explicit way with regard to his behaviour in public (p. 64, ll. 26–28, 31–32), so that it is easy to imagine the effect the commercial glitter of the Big Store has on him (p. 65, ll. 10–14). Though the self-important Manager is portrayed in mildly satirical terms (ll. 17–19, 32), there is no indication that John sees through his pretences. On the contrary (as the incident with the caramel paper shows, ll. 9–10, 15, 20–21), his desire "to please people" (l. 30) is totally uncritical.

In the course of his first day as Father Christmas he gradually acquires some self-confidence, but with frequent relapses. This is described in a series of hilariously comic incidents (e.g. p. 67, l. 22 – p. 68, l. 6; p. 68, ll. 11–15) which culminate in him ringing his bell "with subdued ferocity" in his effort to please everybody. At no time, however, is John seen purely as a figure of fun. Since the reader shares in his thoughts and feelings, the psychological reality of his nervousness and precarious self-confidence is immediately apparent, and one cannot help sympathizing with him.

This is also true of his constant wavering between the urge to rebel and acceptance of his 'fate'. Though Santa's boots are two sizes too small for him, he cannot bring himself to complain to the manager, and instead, exhausts his indignation in private grumbling about his wife's influence over him (p. 66, ll. 13–18, 28–30; p. 68, ll. 16–25). When his internal protests are extended to their logical conclusions, he invariably backs down for fear of unpredictable consequences (p. 68, ll. 20–29; p. 70, ll. 13–20).

The final scene sums up what has emerged in the course of the story of John's personality and domestic situation. A step into a puddle on his way back from the store in the rain is enough to make him (once again) determined to stand up to his wife and let her know what she had let him in for – the ill-fitting boots, the failure of the management to give him something to eat, etc. On arriving home, the children are still not in bed, which makes matters worse. But his wife is well able to manage the situation: she notices "the hard ring in his voice" (p. 70, l. 37), and everything she does is from then on calculated to assuage his anger. The warm socks, the "nice bit of steak", the fresh blouse she puts on, the pipe already filled with tobacco, the roaring fire and a kiss do the trick: "he knew that he would say nothing to her now about the tight boots."

One can interpret this scene as John's final defeat. But the double perspective on the man's conflicting tendencies ensures that objective judgement is tempered with subjective insight. The consolation inherent in John's wife's love and understanding (even if it is in part calculating) comes across clearly. In this tableau of life in a Belfast slum there is a strong suggestion of the Christian origins of the feast of Christmas – a spirit which was totally absent from the world of the Big Store.

First Unit
Exposition and Narrative Point of View

Preparation: Though this unit can be dealt with on the basis of a close reading of the first three pages, it is recommended that the students should have read the whole story.

1. The exposition
How much is conveyed by the first two-and-a-half lines of the story?
Two characters, a man (by implication) and "his wife"; poor living conditions – "newspaper which served as tablecloth"; situation – the man is looking for a job, or at least being encouraged by his wife to do so.
How is this basic information elaborated on, up to line 30?
The couple have two children, who seem in danger of going hungry (ll. 5–6); air of shabby respectability, mainly due to efforts of wife (ll. 11–13, 18–19); some characterization; time of year (ll. 7, 25) and the job to be applied for: 'Father Christmas' in a big store; a hint of the social background – widespread unemployment (ll. 24–30).

2. Narrative technique
What kind of narrator is used to tell the story? What point(s) of view does the narrator adopt? (Consider in particular the paragraph ll. 23–30.)
An 'outside' author/narrator who plays no part in the story itself; shifting viewpoint; dominant perspective – that of the central character. The narrator frequently enters into John's mind, as it were, and presents his thoughts and feelings directly, sometimes in the form of 'substitutionary narration', e.g. p. 66, ll. 17–18, 29–30; p. 68, ll. 10, 24–25).

3. The effect of the 'double' point of view
Consider your personal reaction to the passage where John dresses up in his 'Santa Claus' costume and goes out into the shop (p. 66, ll. 6–30). What effect does the point of view have here?

The reader shares John's pleasure and amusement (ll. 7–8) as well as his nervousness and confusion (ll. 22–30); consequence – sympathy, understanding, opportunity to identify, at least partially, with John.
What prevents full identification with John?
Because of the third-person narrative we see him from the outside as well, and can be critical of his exaggerated nervousness, his "weak and self-conscious" voice (p. 67, l. 4), etc. – or amused (esp. p. 68, ll. 11–15).

Homework: Re-read story (or read to end) and pick out all the passages that make general statements about John's personality – and that of his wife.

Second Unit
Characterization of John and His Wife

1. Direct characterization of John (Discussion of Homework)
What are we told directly about the kind of person John is? Consider also who is telling us this.
P. 64, ll. 26–27: "timid little man" (narrator speaking)
P. 65, l. 30: "he always tried to please people" (could be John's own evaluation of himself)
P. 66, ll. 16–17: "he wasn't one to complain" (probably John speaking)
P. 68, ll. 22–23: "no strength – no power to stand up ..." (John)

2. Indirect characterization of John
How do John's behaviour, feelings and thoughts help to characterize him?
On the whole, they confirm what we are told directly: he does what his wife tells him (p. 64, ll. 1–26) and shows considerable lack of self-confidence (p. 64, ll. 27–28, 31–32; p. 66, ll. 22, 24–28; p. 67, ll. 4, 10–15; p. 68, ll. 5–6). In addition, we learn of his occasional determination to change (p. 68, ll. 24–25; p. 70, ll. 13–17), which, however, never lasts long.

3. Characterization of John's wife (Discussion of homework)
What remarks does John make about his wife? Which seem to be justified?
Two kinds of remarks: complaints about her domination and interference (p. 66, ll. 29–30; p. 70, ll. 1–5), and reflections on her wisdom (p. 65, ll. 1–2; p. 71, ll. 14–16). What is portrayed of her actual behaviour at the beginning and end of the story seems to suggest that both have a certain basis in reality – while definitely dominating him, she shows considerable psychological insight in doing so, she knows her husband's weaknesses, knows how to manage him (cf. in particular last paragraph).

4. John's changing attitude to his wife

Describe the way John's attitude varies between acceptance of his wife's domination and rebellion.

His 'wavering' could be summed up in a kind of 'temperature chart', as follows:

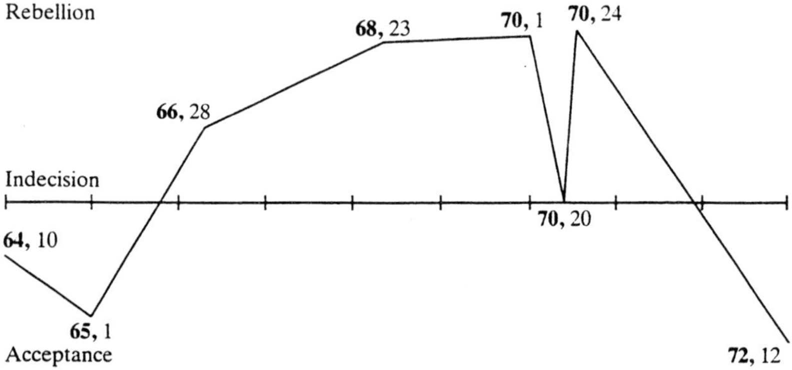

5. Open discussion (or written Homework exercise, to be discussed in the the Third Unit)

How satisfying do you find the ending?

Many reactions possible – from disappointment at John's failure to express his feelings of frustration, to satisfaction at the preservation of peace and harmony. [One object of the discussion should be to stimulate an awareness that different reactions are possible and can even co-exist, having been prepared by the double perspective on John's conflicting tendencies.]

Third Unit
A Christmas Story?

1. Expectations evoked by the title

When you first read the title, what kind of story did you expect?

Some possible expectations: a sentimental 'Christmas story'; a story for or about children; a humorous story; a fairy tale.

To what extent are such expectations realized by the story?

- action takes place at Christmas;
- about a 'Santa Claus', but from an unusual perspective, i.e. not child's point of view;
- plenty of humour, but embedded in a serious story;
- no 'fairy tale', very realistic

2. Implicit criticism of the commercialization of Christmas
What effect does this story of urban poverty have when told against a background of Christmas festivities?
Contrast with the 'tinsel' and the commercial aspects of Christmas emphasizes the family's dreary surroundings (not overdone, however). On the other hand, the family's economic plight makes the commercial glitter seem cheap. The figure of the Manager is mildly satirized: his self-importance, and his overriding interest in increasing profits (p. 65, ll. 17–19, 31–34; p. 66, l. 39 – p. 67, l. 7; p. 69, ll. 30–32). Note in particular the episode on p. 67, l. 22 – p. 68, l. 7, which suggests that John and his family aren't the only poor people being exploited.

3. 'Peace and Good Will'
Can you find a 'Christmas' message in the ending of the story?
(Refer back to the discussion in Second Unit, point 5.) The warmth of the fire, the pipe, John's wife's love and understanding (even if in part calculating) are experienced by the reader as full of consolation. There is a strong suggestion of the Christian origins of the feast, which is totally absent from the world of the Big Store.

For Further Study

Courses/Projects based on this story

1. Stories by Michael McLaverty
"Father Christmas" plus a selection of the following, all from *Collected Short Stories* (Poolbeg paperback, Dublin):
- "Pigeons" – extract included in Topical Texts 19: *Youth – Problems and Challenge* (Klett)
- "The Poteen Maker" – also in *Irish Short Stories* (Longman Imprint)
- "The Wild Duck's Nest"
- "Six Weeks On and Two Ashore"

  } – simplified versions in *Irish Short Stories* (Longman Simplified English Series)

(Alternatively, one could read McLaverty's novel *Call My Brother Back*, Poolbeg paperback, Dublin 1979.)

2. Christmas in Literature
- Charles Dickens, *A Christmas Carol*
- Michael McLaverty, "Father Christmas"
- Dylan Thomas, "A Child's Christmas in Wales" – included in *Modern Life* (Klett)

3. Northern Ireland – the Social and Economic Background

- "Father Christmas"
- Reference books for information on the colonization of Ireland and the industralization of the north-east (look up "Ireland", "Northern Ireland", "Ulster", "Belfast")
- From Topical Texts 16: *Ireland and its Problems* (Klett), texts 14–17, 22
- From the Klett slide series *Dias zur Landeskunde* (Ireland: 56815; Lehrerheft: 5681), slides 25–30

Bibliography

Beck, Warren, *Joyce's Dubliners: Substance, Vision, Art,* Duke University Press, Durham, North Carolina 1969.

Bowen, Zack, *Mary Lavin* (Irish Writers Series), Bucknell University Press, Lewisburg 1975.

Briden, Earl F., "Guests of the Nation: A Final Irony" in *Studies in Short* Fiction, 13 (1976), pp. 79–81.

de Paor, Liam, *Divided Ulster,* Penguin 1970.

Dunn, Douglas, *Two Decades of Irish Writing: A Critical Survey,* Cheadle, Cheshire 1975.

Foster, John, *Forces and Themes in Ulster Fiction,* Belfast 1974.

Garrett, Peter K. (ed.), *Twentieth Century Interpretations of Dubliners,* Englewood Cliffs, New Jersey 1968.

Joyce, James, *Letters* (ed. Stuart Gilbert), London 1966.

Joyce, Stanislaus, *My Brother's Keeper* (ed. Richard Ellman), London 1958.

Kelly, Angeline A., *Liam O'Flaherty the Story-teller,* Macmillan, London 1979.

≈ Introduction and Notes to *The Wave and Other Stories,* Longman Imprint, London 1980.

Lavin, Mary, Introduction to revised edition of *Tales from Bective Bridge,* Poolbeg Press, Dublin 1978.

Leatherwood, A. M., "Joyce's Mythic Method: Structure and Unity in 'An Encounter'" in *Studies in Short Fiction,* 13 (1976), pp. 71–78.

Martin, Augustine, "A Skeleton Key to the Stories of Mary Lavin" in *Studies,* 52 (Winter 1963), pp. 393–406.

≈ "Priest and Artist in Joyce's Early Fiction" in *Anglo-Irish Studies,* II (1976), pp. 69–81.

Matthews, James H., *Frank O'Connor* (Irish Writers Series), Bucknell University Press, Lewisburg 1976.

Mercier, Vivian, "The Irish Short Story and Oral Tradition" in *The Celtic Cross,* University of Purdue Press, Lafayette, Indiana 1964.

Murray, Michael H., "Liam O'Flaherty and the Speaking Voice" in *Studies in Short Fiction,* 5 (Winter 1968), pp. 154–162.

O'Brien, James H., *Liam O'Flaherty* (Irish Writers Series), Bucknell University Press, Lewisburg 1973.

O'Connor, Frank, *The Lonely Voice: A Study of the Short Story,* Macmillan, London 1963.
≈ *An Only Child* (autobiography), Macmillan, London 1962; Pan paperback 1970.
≈ *The Backward Look: A Survey of Irish Literature,* Macmillan, London 1967.
≈ Introduction to *Modern Irish Short Stories,* Oxford University Press 1957.
O'Faolain, Sean, *The Short Story,* London 1948; Mercier paperback, Cork 1972.
≈ *Vive Moi* (autobiography), Boston 1964.
≈ *The Irish,* Penguin paperback 1947; revised edition 1969.
≈ Introduction to his collection of stories, *The Heat of the Sun,* London 1966; Pan paperback 1969.
≈ Introduction to *Stories of Sean O'Faolain,* Penguin paperback 1970.
O'Flaherty, Liam, *Shame the Devil* (autobiography), London 1934.
O Muirithe, Diarmaid, *The English Language in Ireland,* Mercier Press, Cork 1977.
Peterson, Richard F., *Mary Lavin* (Twayne's English authors series), Boston 1978.
≈ "The Circle of Truth: The Stories of Katherine Mansfield and Mary Lavin" in *Modern Fiction Studies,* 24 (1978), pp. 383–394.
Rafroidi, Patrick and Terence Brown (eds.), *The Irish Short Story,* Colin Smythe Ltd., Gerrard's Cross, Buckinghamshire 1979.
Roark, Bobbie Jean, *Mary Lavin: the Local and the Universal,* Dissertation, University of Colorado 1968.
Sheehy, Maurice (ed.), *Michael/Frank: Studies on Frank O'Connor,* Knopf, New York 1969.
Synge, J. M., *The Aran Islands,* London 1907; Oxford University Press paperback 1979.
Wohlgelernter, Maurice, *Frank O'Connor: An Introduction,* Columbia University Press, New York 1977.

Additional Reading List

The following are some suggestions for those who would like to widen their knowledge of the Irish short story in English. Included in the list are some of the most influential early collections, as well as a rather arbitrary selection of contemporary writing. Where possible, paperback editions are listed.

Edith Somerville and Martin Ross, *Some Experiences of an Irish R.M.*, London 1899, reissued 1962 (Faber & Faber).

George Moore, *The Untilled Field,* London 1903, reissued 1976.

Daniel Corkery, *The Stormy Hills,* first published 1929, recently reissued as a paperback, Mercier Press, Cork (undated).

Elizabeth Bowen's Irish Stories, (contains stories first published 1930–1956), Poolbeg paperback, Dublin 1978.

Walter Macken, *The Coll Doll and Other Stories,* Macmillan, London.

James Plunkett, *The Trusting and the Maimed,* New York 1955.

Brian McMahon, *The End of the World and Other Stories* (contains stories first published 1950–1970), Poolbeg paperback, Dublin 1976.

Benedict Kiely, *A Journey to the Seven Streams,* Poolbeg paperback, Dublin 1977.

John McGahern, *Nightlines,* Panther paperback 1973.

Edna O'Brien, *A Scandalous Woman and Other Stories,* Penguin 1976.

Maura Treacy, *Sixpence in Her Shoe,* Poolbeg paperback, Dublin 1977.

Bernard McLaverty, *Secrets and Other Stories,* Blackstaff Press paperback, Belfast 1979.

Julia O'Faolain, *Melancholy Baby and Other Stories,* Poolbeg paperback, Dublin 1978.

Mary Beckett, *A Belfast Woman,* Poolbeg paperback, Dublin 1980.

Paddy No More – Modern Irish Short Stories, Wolfhound Press, Dublin 1978.

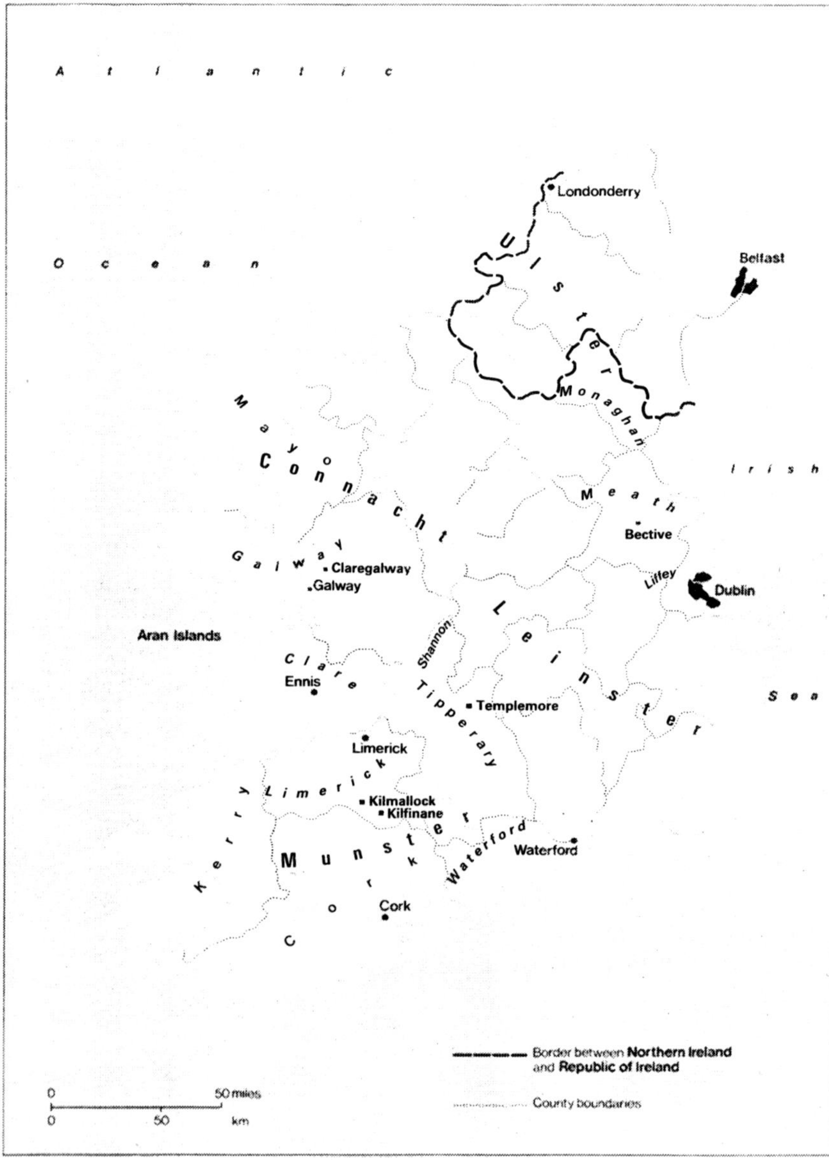
Atlantic Ocean
Londonderry
Ulster
Belfast
Monaghan
Mayo
Connacht
Irish Sea
Meath
Bective
Galway
Claregalway
Galway
Liffey
Dublin
Leinster
Aran Islands
Shannon
Clare
Ennis
Tipperary
Templemore
Limerick
Kerry
Limerick
Kilmallock
Kilfinane
Munster
Cork
Waterford
Waterford
Cork
Border between Northern Ireland and Republic of Ireland
County boundaries
0
50 miles
0
50
km